HOUSING ISSUES, LAWS AND PROGRAMS

MORTGAGES

POLICIES, PROPOSALS AND TRENDS

HOUSING ISSUES, LAWS AND PROGRAMS

Additional books in this series can be found on Nova's website under the Series tab.

Additional E-books in this series can be found on Nova's website under the E-book tab.

ECONOMIC ISSUES, PROBLEMS AND PERSPECTIVES

Additional books in this series can be found on Nova's website under the Series tab.

Additional E-books in this series can be found on Nova's website under the E-book tab.

HOUSING ISSUES, LAWS AND PROGRAMS

MORTGAGES

POLICIES, PROPOSALS AND TRENDS

FOSTER MURPHY
AND
OWEN C. JENSEN
EDITORS

nova publishers
New York

For permission to use material from this book please contact us:
Telephone 631-231-7269; Fax 631-231-8175
Web Site: http://www.novapublishers.com

Library of Congress Cataloging-in-Publication Data

ISBN: 978-1-62257-689-0

Published by Nova Science Publishers, Inc. † New York

CONTENTS

PREFACE

Congressional interest in residential mortgage markets has increased following the collapse of the housing bubble, government financial support to the mortgage market, and housing's perceived importance to the broader economic recovery. Since 2008, the residential mortgage market has experienced some of the highest default and foreclosure rates since the Great Depression. This book provides an overview of the changing residential mortgage market, focusing on trends in housing prices, homeownership, mortgage characteristics, and financing. It also examines legislation and regulations designed to promote the efficient functioning of the mortgage market.

Chapter 1 - This report provides an overview of the changing residential mortgage market, focusing on trends in housing prices, homeownership, mortgage characteristics, and financing. It also examines legislation and regulations designed to promote the efficient functioning of the mortgage market.

Chapter 2 - High default and foreclosure rates in the housing market have resulted in questions as to whether borrowers were fully informed about the terms of their mortgage loans. A lack of transparency with respect to loan terms and settlement costs can make it difficult for consumers to make well-informed decisions when choosing mortgage products. In addition, inadequate disclosures can make some borrowers more vulnerable to predatory lending or discriminatory practices.

The adequate disclosure of mortgage terms is a longstanding issue that has prompted several congressional actions. For example, the Truth in Lending Act (TILA) of 1968 and the Real Estate Settlement Procedures Act (RESPA) of 1974 were enacted to require disclosures of credit costs and terms to borrowers. The Economic Growth and Regulatory Paperwork Reduction Act of 1996 (P.L. 104-208) directed the Federal Reserve Board and the Department of Housing and Urban Development (HUD) to propose a single form that satisfied the requirements of RESPA and TILA. However, the Federal Reserve Board and HUD concluded that regulatory changes would not be sufficient and that further statutory changes would be required for the forms to be consolidated. More recently, the Dodd-Frank Wall Street Reform and Consumer Protection Act of 2010 (Dodd-Frank Act; P.L. 111-203), which established the Consumer Financial Protection Bureau (CFPB), mandated the new agency revisit disclosure stipulations for mortgage loans. In addition, the Dodd-Frank Act requires the CFPB to consolidate mandatory TILA and RESPA disclosures into one Loan Estimate form.

The 112th Congress has been closely monitoring the subsequent rulemaking associated with the Dodd-Frank Act, as well as the performance and effectiveness of the CFPB. Consequently, this report examines one of the first major actions undertaken by the new agency. Specifically, efforts by the CFPB to create an effective mortgage disclosure form for borrowers are discussed.

Chapter 3 - Prior to the recent financial crisis, mortgage underwriting standards were relaxed to the point where many borrowers could only repay their loans if favorable financial conditions that existed at the time of origination remained intact. In other words, borrowers obtained mortgage loans that relied upon interest rates not rising or the value of the underlying collateral (house prices) not declining. When market conditions changed, however, many mortgage loans became delinquent and went into default. The mortgage defaults often translated into large losses for both the borrowers and the financial industry.

After enactment of The Dodd-Frank Wall Street Reform and Consumer Protection Act of 2010 (Dodd-Frank Act; P.L. 111-203), the Federal Reserve Board announced a proposed qualified mortgage (QM) rule that would establish "ability to repay" standards for mortgage lending. The Federal Reserve, along with other federal regulatory agencies, also jointly released a proposed risk retention or qualified residential mortgage (QRM) rule to require parties involved in a transaction in which mortgage originations are sold to retain "skin-in-the-game" or a minimum percentage of the credit risk of financial products, which would result in the sharing of any eventual losses. Adoption of ability to repay and risk-retention standards may discourage lenders from excessively relaxing lending standards even during economic boom periods, thus making loan repayment more resilient to sudden shifts in short-term economic and financial conditions.

The ability to repay and risk-retention standards, while designed to curtail the pre-crisis proliferation of risky lending practices, are likely to simultaneously reduce access to mortgage credit. Although ability-to-repay standards would encourage consistent underwriting at all times, some borrowers that benefit from lender flexibility during more favorable macroeconomic conditions are likely to face increased difficulty obtaining mortgage loans. Lenders may be reluctant to originate loans that are not in compliance with the ability-to-repay standards if this exposes them to increased legal risks. Likewise, risk-retention standards that translate into more stringent qualification requirements for borrowers are likely to increase barriers to homeownership for both creditworthy and disadvantaged borrowers.

The 112th Congress is overseeing the rulemaking stemming from the Dodd-Frank Act. This report examines the developments associated with the implementation of mortgage lending reforms. After summarizing the proposed ability to repay and risk-retention standards, a description of risky underwriting practices that occurred prior to the mortgage crisis is presented, followed by a discussion of possible effects on mortgage credit accessibility.

The Consumer Financial Protection Bureau (CFPB), which will prescribe final regulations on QM rule, has re-opened the comment period to seek further comments on the litigation risks that could potentially arise from the new requirements. The comments, however, should be narrowly focused and based upon analysis that uses mortgage data provided by the regulator of Fannie Mae and Freddie Mac. The closing date for comments will be July 9, 2012.

Chapter 4 - A home foreclosure, mortgage default, or mortgage modification can have important tax consequences. As lenders and borrowers work to resolve indebtedness issues, some transactions are resulting in cancellation of debt. Mortgage debt cancellation can occur when lenders restructure loans, reducing principal balances, or sell properties, either in advance, or as a result, of foreclosure proceedings. Historically, if a lender forgives or cancels such debt, tax law has treated it as cancellation of debt (COD) income subject to tax. Exceptions have been available for taxpayers who are insolvent or in bankruptcy, among others—these taxpayers may exclude canceled mortgage debt income under existing law.

The Mortgage Forgiveness Debt Relief Act of 2007, P.L. 110-142, signed into law on December 20, 2007, temporarily excludes qualified COD income.

Thus, the act allows taxpayers who do not qualify for the existing exceptions to exclude COD income. The provision is effective for debt discharged before January 1, 2010. The Emergency Economic Stabilization Act of 2008, P.L. 110-343, extends the exclusion of COD income to debt discharged before January 1, 2013. Most recently, several bills have been introduced in the 112th Congress that would extend the exclusion of COD income again. H.R. 4336 would extend the exclusion through 2013, S. 2250 and H.R. 4202 would extend the exclusion through 2014, and H.R. 4250 and H.R. 4290 would extend the exclusion through 2015.

A rationale for excluding canceled mortgage debt income has focused on minimizing hardship for households in distress. Policymakers have expressed concern that households experiencing hardship and that are in danger of losing their home, presumably as a result of financial distress, should not incur an additional hardship by being taxed on canceled debt income. Some analysts have also drawn a connection between minimizing hardship for individuals and consumer spending; reductions in consumer spending, if significant, can lead to recession.

As efforts to minimize the rate of foreclosure are being made, lenders are, in some cases, renegotiating loans with borrowers to keep them in the home. For some policymakers, the exclusion of canceled mortgage debt income may be a necessary step to ensure that homeowner retention efforts are not thwarted by tax policy.

Opponents of an exclusion for canceled mortgage debt income might argue that the provision would make debt forgiveness more attractive for homeowners, and could encourage homeowners to be less responsible about fulfilling debt obligations.

Mortgage debt cancellation occurs when lenders engage in loss-mitigation solutions that either (1) restructure the loan and reduce the principal balance or (2) sell the property, either in advance, or as a result of foreclosure proceedings. Under current law, the canceled debt (sometimes referred to as discharge of indebtedness) may be income subject to taxation.

The Mortgage Forgiveness Debt Relief Act of 2007, P.L. 110-142, signed into law on December 20, 2007, temporarily excludes qualified COD income. Thus, the act allows taxpayers who do not qualify for the existing exceptions to exclude COD income. The provision is effective for debt discharged before January 1, 2010. The Emergency Economic Stabilization Act of 2008, P.L. 110-343, extends the exclusion of COD income to debt discharged before January 1, 2013. Most recently, several bills have been introduced in the 112th Congress that would extend the exclusion of COD income again. H.R. 4336 would extend the exclusion through 2013, S. 2250 and H.R. 4202 would extend the exclusion through 2014, and H.R. 4250 and H.R. 4290 would extend the exclusion through 2015.

The rationales for this change are to minimize hardship for households in distress and to ensure that non-tax-related homeowner retention efforts are not thwarted by tax policy. Critics argue that the exclusion could encourage homeowners to be less responsible about fulfilling debt obligations.[2] Critics may also argue that owner-occupied housing is sufficiently subsidized even without a COD income exclusion.

This report begins with an overview and analysis of the historical tax treatment of canceled debt income. Next, the changes enacted by P.L. 110-142 and P.L. 110-343 are discussed. A discussion of policy options concludes.

Chapter 5 - The bursting of the housing bubble in 2006 precipitated the December 2007-June 2009 recession and a financial panic in September 2008. With the housing market seen as a locus for many of the economic problems that emerged, some Members of Congress propose intervening in the housing market as a means of improving not only the housing market itself but also the financial sector and the broader economy. Critics are concerned that further intervention could prolong the housing slump, delay recovery, and affect outcomes based on the government's preferences rather than market forces.

This report provides a brief overview of policy proposals for the large-scale refinancing of mortgages for borrowers shut out of traditional financing methods.

Chapter 6 - The United States single-family housing market has $10.5 trillion of mortgage debt outstanding. Servicers play an important role in this market. The owner of a mortgage loan or mortgage-backed security typically hires a servicer to act on its behalf. When loans are current, a mortgage servicer collects payments from borrowers and forwards them to the mortgage holders. If the borrower becomes delinquent, a servicer may offer the borrower an option that could allow the borrower to stay in his or her home, or the servicer may pursue foreclosure.

Following high foreclosure rates and recent allegations of abuse, mortgage servicing has attracted attention from Congress. In addition to hearings and congressional investigations, some in Congress have called for national servicing standards. The most comprehensive proposal, S. 824, the Foreclosure Fraud and Homeowner Abuse Prevention Act of 2011 (Senator Sherrod Brown et al.), and its companion bill in the House, H.R. 1783 (Representative Brad Miller et al.), contain provisions intended to protect investors and borrowers from improper servicing practices. S. 967, the

Regulation of Mortgage Servicing Act of 2011 (Senator Jeff Merkley et al.), includes borrower protections in addition to those offered by S. 824 and H.R. 1783.

The servicing standards proposed in S. 824 and H.R. 1783 include provisions intended to ensure that servicers act in the best interest of investors who hold mortgage loans. The proposals would adjust the servicing compensation structure to better align servicer incentives with the incentives of the mortgage holder. Servicers would also be prohibited from purchasing services offered by their affiliates at inflated costs and passing the costs on to investors. In addition, servicers would be prohibited from choosing a loss mitigation option that would benefit their affiliates at the expense of other investors.

S. 824, H.R. 1783, and S. 967 have three major components for borrower protection. First, the three bills would require servicers to establish a single point of contact with the borrower. The single point of contact would be a case manager who is assigned to each delinquent borrower and would manage communications with the borrower. Second, the three bills would prohibit servicers from dual tracking, which means initiating foreclosure on a borrower while simultaneously pursuing a loan modification. Servicers would instead be required to determine whether the borrower is eligible for an alternative to foreclosure before initiating foreclosure. Third, S. 824 and H.R. 1783 would set minimum experience, education, and training levels for loan modification staff and limit caseload levels for individual employees.

Legislation is not the only avenue to setting servicing standards. Regulatory agencies, such as the Consumer Financial Protection Bureau, the Board of Governors of the Federal Reserve System, and the Federal Deposit Insurance Corporation, may include some or all of the proposed standards in their rules on securitization and qualified residential mortgages pursuant to the Dodd-Frank Wall Street Reform and Consumer Protection Act (P.L. 111-203). Servicing standards could also be adopted through legal settlements between the servicers and the state attorneys general, as well as through enforcement actions taken by federal regulators in response to deficient servicing practices by some banks. If servicing standards are implemented by rule or by settlement agreements, they would apply only to those servicers under the regulators' purview or those who entered into the settlement agreements.

In: Mortgages: Policies, Proposals and Trends ISBN: 978-1-62257-689-0
Editors: F. Murphy and O. C. Jensen

Chapter 1

CHANGES TO THE RESIDENTIAL MORTGAGE MARKET: LEGISLATION, DEMOGRAPHICS, AND OTHER DRIVERS*

N. Eric Weiss

SUMMARY

This report provides an overview of the changing residential mortgage market, focusing on trends in housing prices, homeownership, mortgage characteristics, and financing. It also examines legislation and regulations designed to promote the efficient functioning of the mortgage market.

Congressional Concern about Mortgages

Congressional interest in residential mortgage markets has increased following the collapse of the housing bubble, government financial support to the mortgage market, and housing's perceived importance to the broader economic recovery. Since 2008, the residential mortgage market has experienced some of the highest default and foreclosure rates since the Great Depression. The future of Fannie Mae and Freddie Mac, two congressionally

* This is an edited, reformatted and augmented version of the Congressional Research Service Publication, CRS Report for Congress R42571, dated June 19, 2012.

chartered government-sponsored enterprises (GSEs) that have long been central pillars of the mortgage market, is also the subject of congressional debate. Both GSEs are currently in conservatorship and being supported financially by the U.S. Department of the Treasury. There is also concern over the financial conditions of the Federal Housing Administration's (FHA's) mortgage guarantee program.

How Mortgages Are Funded

Today and in the foreseeable future, home mortgages are indirectly financed by financial institutions such as pension funds, college endowments, central banks, and sovereign wealth funds. A household seeking a mortgage typically applies directly to an organization (or part of a larger organization) that specializes in the mortgage origination process. This mortgage originator uses credit scores and computer systems to underwrite (evaluate) the mortgage application. The originator may "hold the mortgage in portfolio" as an investment or sell it within days of being issued. In the latter case, the mortgage might be sold again, and typically ends up pooled with other mortgages in a mortgage-backed security (MBS) that is guaranteed by Fannie Mae, Freddie Mac, or by the federal government through Ginnie Mae, which is part of the Department of Housing and Urban Development (HUD). The MBS frequently is sold to an institutional investor. In many cases servicing is contracted out and the homeowner does not know who actually owns the mortgage.

Possible Changes to the Residential Mortgage Market

Change is expected on a variety of fronts.

- More than 45 bills such as H.R. 31, H.R. 408, H.R. 463, H.R. 1182, H.R. 1221, H.R. 1222, H.R. 1223, H.R. 1224, H.R. 1225, H.R. 1226, H.R. 1227, H.R. 1859, H.R. 2413, H.R. 2425, H.R. 2428, H.R. 2436, H.R. 2439, H.R. 2440, H.R. 2441, H.R. 2462, S. 178, and S. 693 have been introduced to enhance the accountability of Fannie Mae and Freddie Mac. Some of the bills seek to reduce the cost to the government, while others seek to change the enterprises' charters if or when they leave conservatorship. None of the listed bills introduced proposes government actions to replace the two enterprises.

- Previously enacted legislation requires regulations for full implementation. For example, the Dodd-Frank Wall Street Reform and Consumer Protection Act (Dodd-Frank Act; P.L. 111-203) requires new regulations affecting risk retention and mandating that mortgages be "suitable" for borrowers.
- Legislation has been introduced to establish national mortgage servicing standards.
- The maximum size of mortgages that can be purchased by Fannie Mae or Freddie Mac, or included in mortgage-backed securities (MBSs) guaranteed by Ginnie Mae (part of the FHA) with the full faith and credit of the U.S. government, has been changed by legislation six times since 2008. Five bills have been introduced in the 112th Congress (H.R. 408, S. 178, H.R. 1182, S. 693, and H.R. 1859) that would make additional changes to the loan limit.
- Independent of legislation, demographics, the recent recession, and the experience of the housing bubble are likely to result in changes to household formation and homeownership preferences.

CHANGES IN THE RESIDENTIAL MORTGAGE MARKET

For many years, homeownership has been promoted as part of the American dream. Over the last 50 years, the homeownership rate has been in the range of 62% to 66%. Since 2008, however, the residential mortgage market has experienced historically high default and foreclosure rates, credit losses, liquidity problems, and tighter mortgage standards.

In addition, Fannie Mae and Freddie Mac, two congressionally chartered government-sponsored enterprises (GSEs) formed to provide liquidity and access to the mortgage market, have been placed in conservatorship and are being supported by the U.S. Department of the Treasury and the Federal Reserve.[1]

In 2011, Fannie Mae and Freddie Mac together owned or securitized 46.7% of the $11.4 trillion residential mortgage market.[2] Some have questioned the solvency of the mortgage insurance program of the Federal Housing Administration (FHA).

For some households, the financial risk implied by the experience of nationwide house price declines may make renting more attractive relative to owning a home. It is not clear that today's most popular type of mortgage, the 30-year fixed rate, will continue as the most popular or even exist.

In coming years, the residential mortgage market is likely to change in response to legislation, regulatory actions, demographic changes, and continuing problems in the mortgage market.[3] These changes may be of interest to Congress because of the impact on current and future homeowners, the real estate and home building industries, and the financial system.

Changes to the mortgage market can be organized into three categories: legislative, regulatory, and demographic.

Legislative Changes

Congress is considering legislation that would change the residential mortgage market.

- Fannie Mae and Freddie Mac could be affected by more than 45 bills that have been introduced. These bills would require various changes to the GSEs, including possible elimination, executive compensation, decreasing risk in their investment portfolios, reducing their issuance of new bonds, modifying affordable housing goals, prohibiting new products, restricting the payment of legal fees, requiring the sale of assets, and removing their exemption from certain state and local taxes. These changes would reduce or eliminate the GSEs' role in supplying mortgage funds, but it is likely that the private sector would replace at least some of the funding that Fannie Mae and Freddie Mac currently provide. Legislation has been introduced to change the home mortgage market in the areas of refinancing, foreclosures, fraud prevention, and mortgage servicing.[4]
- H.R. 940, the United States Covered Bond Act of 2011, which would encourage issuing a competitive type of securitization, covered bonds, was introduced in the112th Congress by Representative Scott Garrett.[5] A covered bond is a type of bond issued by a company that contracts to make scheduled interest payments. Specific mortgages are set aside as collateral for the bonds in the event that the issuer does not make the interest payments.

- Other bills (e.g., S. 1963) have been introduced to create a temporary government agency to replace the GSEs with a full faith and credit guarantee of timely payment of principal and interest to holders of mortgage-backed securities (MBSs). This new agency would replace Fannie Mae's and Freddie Mac's similar corporate guarantees and at least partially offset the reduction in the supply of mortgage funds.
- To increase tax revenues, the National Commission on Fiscal Responsibility and Reform (sometimes called Bowles-Simpson) proposed reducing the tax deduction for mortgage interest paid on principal and second residences.[6] In isolation, these proposals could reduce the demand for mortgages and homeownership, and could reduce the price per square foot of homes, the overall price of homes, and the size of new homes.[7]
- The maximum unpaid balance on mortgages purchased by Fannie Mae or Freddie Mac, or guaranteed by the Federal Housing Administration (FHA) and Ginnie Mae (part of the HUD) with the full faith and credit of the U.S. government, has been changed by legislation six times since 2008. Higher limits increase the supply of low-risk mortgage funding, reducing the interest rate on mortgages affected, and increasing the prices of homes affected.[8] Five bills have been introduced in the 112th Congress (H.R. 408, S. 178, H.R. 1182, S. 693, and H.R. 1859) that would make additional changes to the loan limit.
- In February 2011, the Obama Administration issued a report[9] with three general proposals to reform the housing finance system including FHA, Fannie Mae, and Freddie Mac. These proposals would reduce the government's support for the mortgage markets. Some who purchase MBSs because of the government's support are likely to switch from the GSEs' MBSs to safer investments, and other classes of investors could be attracted to the higher risk associated with higher mortgage market returns. It is not clear what the net effect on mortgage markets might be.
- There are similar proposals to reform the Federal Housing Administration's (FHA's) mortgage guarantee program.

New Regulations

Government agencies are developing new regulations that will affect the mortgage market.

- The Dodd-Frank Wall Street Reform and Consumer Protection Act (Dodd-Frank Act; P.L. 111-203) requires the Consumer Finance Protection Board to adopt regulations[10] to implement "qualified residential mortgages" (QRMs)[11] and "qualified mortgages" (QMs),[12] which would affect risk retention, underwriting, pooling, and selling the mortgages as MBSs.
- The Consumer Financial Protection Bureau is developing procedures to review lenders' mortgage servicing procedures and to establish uniform rules concerning record keeping and minimum notice of interest rate increases.[13]
- FHFA, the Fed, and FDIC have proposed regulations affecting the capital (reserves) that insured depositories must hold against mortgages,[14] and using covered bonds[15] to finance mortgages. The Federal Reserve wrote to the House and Senate committees with jurisdiction over housing finance suggesting additional government interventions in the housing finance system to provide new support for the sector.[16]

Demographics and Other Drivers of Change

Demographics and related factors are changing demand for housing and thus mortgage markets.

- Based on past relationships, the demographics of a maturing population suggest an increase in the homeownership rate,[17] but other factors such as movement to assisted living facilities might offset this.[18] Immigration increases the demand for housing, but the impact on homeownership rates could vary depending on the immigrants' income, planned length of stay in the United States, and their attitude towards home owning.[19]
- Tighter mortgage qualification standards could reduce the homeownership rate compared to what it otherwise could be.[20]

- The ability and desire to own a home may have declined for many who have lost their homes due to foreclosure or faced the threat of foreclosure, and this could change historical patterns of homeownership. Other households could also reassess the risks of foreclosure and may decide not to purchase a home.
- Additional, unpredictable factors affecting homeownership rates include the state of the economy, interest rates, inflation, and expectations for the future (including home price expectations). If these change, homeownership rates could change. In particular, rates for 30-year fixed-rate mortgages have been around 4% while inflation has been 1.5% to 3.0%, making real (inflation-adjusted) mortgage rates 1% to 2.5%. While real mortgage rates have been low by historical standards, if the economy weakens, and house prices continue to decline, households may continue to defer home purchases.

The net result on homeownership rates is unclear: they could rise or fall.

Overview of Residential Mortgage Markets

A home is an infrequent consumer purchase that combines consumption, investment, and a variety of risks. Financing the purchase of a home with a mortgage adds a level of financial complexity and risk, but allows a purchaser to better match the flow of housing services with the flow of paying for the capital that provides the services.

Homes are most frequently financed with 30-year fixed-rate mortgages that historically have been paid off in 7-10 years usually by refinancing the mortgage or by selling the home. The demand for owner-occupied homes and associated mortgages depends on a wide variety of factors: home prices, household credit history, the cost of renting housing, mortgage interest rates, mortgage characteristics, household formation, household income, and age, to name some of the most important.

Expected changes in house prices, income, household size, and government incentives are important. The supply of owner-occupied homes and mortgages depends on many factors: the price of existing housing; the cost of land, labor, and materials; interest rates; and the characteristics of alternative investments.

Mortgages are characterized by their interest rate, their term (life), the allocation of payments to principal and interest, the frequency of payments, and adjustments, if any, to the interest rate.

Risk

As a financial instrument, a mortgage is characterized by a flow of interest payments, repayment of principal, and various types of risk. There are many ways to categorize risk. This report concentrates on three types of risk: credit, prepayment, and interest rate. *Credit risk* is the risk that the borrower will not make the payments specified in the mortgage. In general terms, the credit risk of a mortgage to the borrower and to the lender depends on the probability of delinquency, the probability of going to foreclosure following delinquency, possible losses from foreclosure sales, and possible recovery from other assets of the borrower. Federal programs to encourage homeownership over renting have reduced the cost of homeownership by allowing homeowners tax deductions that renters cannot take.[21] Also, government and private sector programs offer insurance and loan guarantees that limit the loss to lenders in the event of foreclosure.

Prepayment risk is the risk that borrowers will pay off the mortgage before the full term (e.g., 30 years). This manifests itself in unanticipated prepayments when interest rates decline and borrowers take advantage of the savings from refinancing. Lenders anticipate a certain prepayment speed and seek an interest rate to compensate, but long-term forecasts of future interest rates are notoriously inaccurate. When the prepayment rate is greater than expected, the lender must find replacement investments at lower interest rates. Conversely, when interest rates increase, prepayment speeds decline, and lenders find their funds tied up in mortgages for longer than anticipated.

Interest rate risk is incurred by lenders that finance long-term fixed interest rate mortgages by repeatedly borrowing for short periods of time at fluctuating interest rates. Lenders typically borrow some or all of the funds used to make a mortgage. As a simple example, a bank might finance a 30-year mortgage loan through shorter-term certificates of deposit (CDs). The difference, or spread, between the short-term interest rate on the CDs and the rate on the mortgages covers the cost of the mortgage and provides the lender with profits. If short-term interest rates on the CDs increase, the profit declines and may become a loss.

Funding Sources

Home mortgages have changed significantly since 1934 when the National Housing Act (P.L. 73-479) created the Federal Housing Administration (FHA) to insure home mortgages. At that time, there were many restrictions on mortgage lending that have since been abolished. For example, banks could not lend on property more than 50 miles from the one office they were allowed. A homeowner usually would apply to a lender, which would use its own standards to decide whether to make the loan. Although some loans were sold to other financial institutions, the lender usually held it and serviced it until it was paid off.

Today, homeowners seeking a mortgage apply to a mortgage originator, which may or may not be part of a larger financial organization. The originator reviews (underwrites) the mortgage application and approves it, frequently according to criteria established by government agencies such as FHA or quasi-government agencies such as Fannie Mae, Freddie Mac, and the Federal Home Loan Banks.

The originator typically sells the mortgage to a securitizer, which pools them into mortgage-backed securities (MBSs) that are in turn sold to institutional investors including trusts, pension funds, and sovereign wealth funds. Sometimes an originator or a securitizer will keep mortgages in its investment portfolio.

Securitization has potential benefits and costs. Among the benefits is that it has made financial markets more efficient. There appear to be many economies of scale in these operations. The originator specializes in marketing to consumers and underwriting. Another organization can specialize in servicing loans by collecting and recording payments, and forwarding the funds to investors.

A standardized security can be traded more easily than one that is unique. This in turn opens financial markets to funding by institutional investors who have no desire to develop the capability to perform all of these functions.

Among the costs of securitization are potential conflicts of interest among originators, investors, and servicers. Renegotiating the terms of a mortgage can be complicated depending on the contracts between the servicer, securitizer, and investors. If renegotiation is considered "active" management, the favorable treatment of MBSs as untaxed pass-throughs can be lost.

Prior to the recent financial crisis, mortgage securitization was done by one of three types of organizations: Ginnie Mae, Fannie Mae/Freddie Mac, and so-called private-label securitizers (PLS).

- Ginnie Mae,[22] which is part of the Department of Housing and Urban Development (HUD), authorizes the securitization of mortgages in its name and guarantees mortgages that already are guaranteed by the federal government (i.e., the Federal Housing Administration [FHA], the Department of Veterans' Agency [VA], or the Department of Agriculture's Rural Housing program). Both the mortgage guarantees to lenders and the MBS guarantee to investors are backed by the full faith and credit of the federal government. Technically, Ginnie Mae never owns the mortgages or the MBSs. The mortgages are purchased and securitized by authorized investment banks.
- Fannie Mae and Freddie Mac,[23] two congressionally chartered, stockholder-owned government-sponsored enterprises (GSEs), purchase and securitize mortgages that meet their standards and certain legal requirements. They either hold the MBSs as an investment or sell them to others. The GSEs cannot purchase mortgages that are larger than the conforming loan limit[24] and must state that their MBSs and bonds are not guaranteed by the federal government.[25]
- Private label securitizations (PLS) have no guarantees (government or otherwise). Typically, these mortgages are securitized by investment banks because they exceed the conforming loan limit, or do not meet other credit requirements of Ginnie or the GSEs. Although PLS were popular in the years preceding the 2008 financial crisis, there has been very little PLS activity since then.[26]

Figure 1 graphs the financing of outstanding mortgages and shows the increasing role of MBSs and the GSEs since the data were first collected in 1952. Initially, this was all done by Fannie Mae, which was a government agency at the time. The first private-label securitizations occurred in 1984, and volume peaked in 2007. Since 2007, the volume of PLS outstanding has declined, reflecting virtually no new PLS issues. The figure shows that while there is a virtual lack of new PLS, there are still PLS outstanding.

Government involvement in the mortgage market is increasing. Fannie Mae and Freddie Mac, which own or guarantee approximately half of all mortgages outstanding, are in federal conservatorship and have received more than $187 billion in support from the U.S. Treasury.[27] The Federal Reserve (Fed) and Treasury have purchased more than $1,347 billion of mortgage-backed securities issued by Fannie and Freddie. The Fed currently is using repayment of mortgages to purchase additional MBSs while Treasury has sold the $225 billion of MBSs that it purchased in 2008 and 2009.[28] The Fed has purchased more than $34 billion of debt issued by Fannie Mae and Freddie Mac.

1952-2011

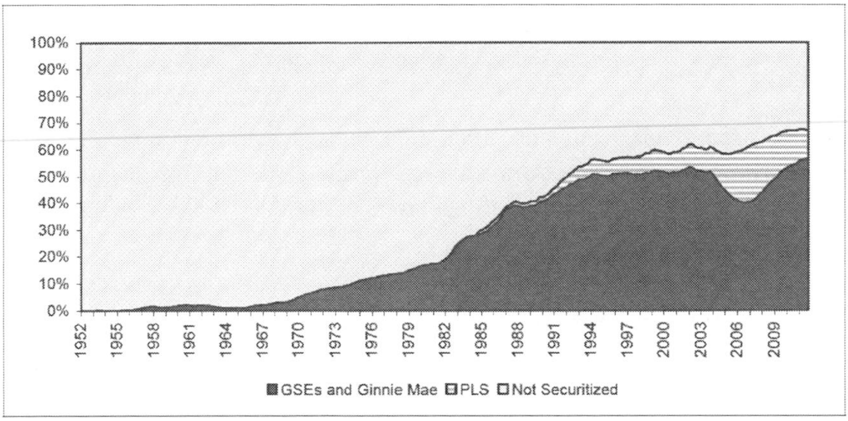

Source: Federal Reserve, "Table L. 218, Home Mortgages," *Flow of Funds: Historical Data*, March 8, 2012, available at http://www.federalreserve.gov/releases/z1/.

Note: Given the available data, CRS cannot separate MBSs issued by Ginnie Mae from those issued by Fannie Mae and Freddie Mac.

Figure 1. Growth of Mortgage Securitization Outstanding.

In oversight hearings, the House Committee on Financial Services[29] and the Senate Committee on Banking, Housing, and Urban Affairs[30] have held hearings on the potential cost of the government's intervention in the mortgage market, conservatorship, and other issues related to the GSEs.

Congressional interest is not limited to Fannie Mae and Freddie Mac. The House Committee on Financial Services held a hearing on December 1, 2011, to examine the financial risks presented by the Federal Housing Administration's single-family insurance program.[31]

HOMEOWNERSHIP AND HOUSE PRICE CHANGES

Changes to the supply and demand for housing and mortgages may be driven by many factors such as the age distribution of households, household formation rate, interest rates, and how rents affect the supply and demand for homeownership. The net effects will be observable through the movements of prices and quantities—house prices and the ownership of homes. This section examines the evolution of house prices and how these trend against other measures that have been of interest to policy makers.

Homeownership Rates

In the period between 1900 and 1940, the homeownership rate varied between 44% and 48%. In 1950, the first data available after World War II, the rate increased to 55%, and since 1960 the rate has been in the range of 62% to 66%.[32] The nation's highest homeownership rate exceeded this range to reach 69.2% in both the second and fourth quarters of 2004.

Cost of Homeownership

The net cost of homeownership is the cost of interest, taxes, depreciation, maintenance expenses, and any price appreciation.[33] In making the decision whether to own or rent a home, the flow of these costs can be compared with the expect flow of benefits from homeownership, the cost of renting, and the benefits of renting.

Because of the transaction costs associated with moving, buying a home, and selling it, households adjust to housing market changes slowly.

From the household's point of view, rising house prices reduced the cost of homeownership, in some cases making the cost negative. Prior to the 2007-2009 financial crisis, nationwide nominal house prices had risen with minor exceptions since 1942, encouraging the formation of the expectation that national house prices could not decline. This arguably led to overestimations of the profitability of homeownership.[34]

Figure 2 shows the nominal and real Case-Shiller home price indices, which hold quality constant.[35] An examination of the real home prices (the solid, dark blue line) shows numerous price declines, that is, periods when house prices did not keep up with inflation.

On average across the entire United States, housing has not always protected homeowners from inflation. Real home prices show a relatively small upward trend prior to 2000.

Although nominal home prices (the dotted, red line) show a stronger upward trend, there have been years when they declined. Between 1890 and 1945, there were a total of 21 years when nominal house prices declined. More recently, between 1945 and 1960, there were 5 years with declines. The next annual, nationwide nominal price decline was in 1990. Except for the first and second quarters of 2010, the price index has declined quarterly since the third quarter of 2006.

Changing Home Prices

Easing credit standards can increase the demand for homeownership and increase home prices. Households that otherwise would be unable to borrow can become homeowners.

Households that would have qualified to purchase under tighter lending standards can buy more expensive housing. In the extreme case, rapidly rising prices make it difficult or impossible for some first-time homebuyers to accumulate sufficient savings for a downpayment, and income may not increase fast enough to keep up with the monthly mortgage payments required for increasingly expensive homes.

From the lender's point of view, rising nominal house prices can be good because the value of the individual home that is the collateral for the mortgage increases. This reduces both the likelihood and severity of any losses in the event of foreclosure.

A foreclosure is less likely when a home is worth more than the mortgage(s) on it, because a delinquent homeowner can sell the house, pay off the mortgage(s), walk away with cash, and avoid foreclosure. If a foreclosure does occur, losses are likely to be less because of the price increase.

Rising home prices allow homeowners to borrow against their increased equity (the difference between the value of a home and the debt on it) through second mortgages (mortgages that have a claim on the home as collateral that is secondary to the original mortgage) and home equity lines of credit (HELOCs). This borrowing can allow for increased consumer spending, which boosts the macro economy.

When nominal house price appreciation slows or begins to decline, the economics of homeownership are reversed.

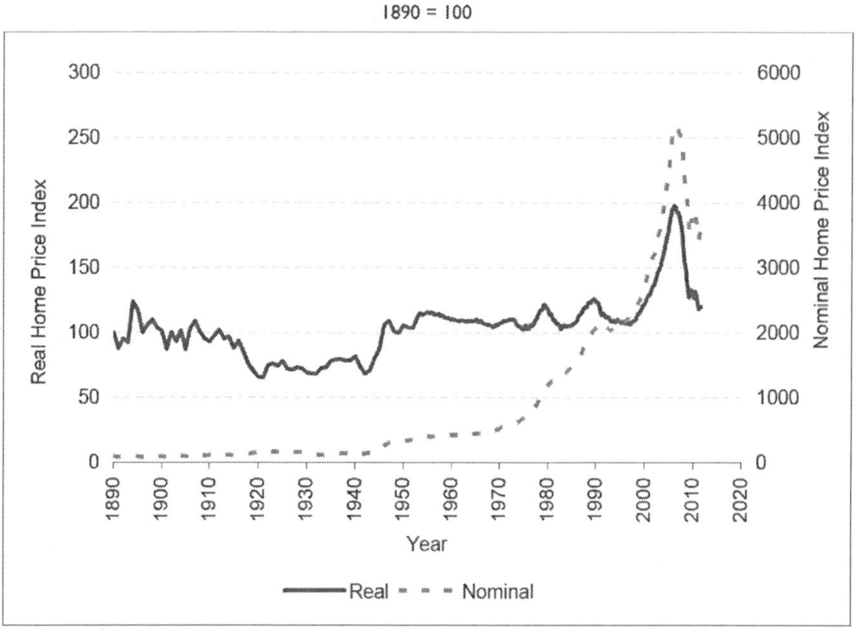

Source: Robert Shiller, *Irrational Exuberance*, Second ed. (Princeton, NJ: Broadway Books, 2005). Numbers updated by the author. Available at http://www.econ.yale.edu/~shiller/data/Fig2-1.xls.

Figure 2. Real and Nominal Home Price Index.

CHANGES IN MORTGAGE CHARACTERISTICS

Since the Depression of the 1930s, mortgages have been characterized by long terms (20 to 30 years), fixed interest rates, prepayment of mortgages without penalty, decreased downpayment requirements, increased standardization, and some type of government insurance for lenders.

Although the 30-year fixed-rate mortgage (FRM) currently is the most popular mortgage (84% of all first mortgages),[36] borrowers have many alternatives. In 1982, the Garn-St. Germain Act[37] pre-empted state laws to permit adjustable-rate mortgages (ARMs), which are tied to various interest rates and with various limits on annual and lifetime interest rate changes.[38] FRMs and ARMs usually have loan terms of 15 to 40 years. Today, downpayments typically range from 3% to more than 40%, and credit standards are higher compared to before the recent recession.

ARMs are not very common. In 2009, slightly over 4% of all home mortgages outstanding were reported to have adjustable rates.[39] Economic research has suggested that the reason for ARMs' lack of acceptance is that consumers find that the initial lower rate on ARMs compared to FRMs does not compensate for the risk that the ARM rate could exceed the FRM rate in the future and that this reflects the interest rate differences on short- and long-term Treasury bonds,[40] that is, short-term interest rates are not sufficiently lower than long-term rates to make the ARMs attractive.

The greater complexity of ARMs may encourage many homeowners to select the simpler FRM.

Despite the low market share for ARMs, they can be advantageous under certain circumstances. One such instance is when the interest rate on ARMs is sufficiently lower than the rate on FRMs. This can occur when there is great uncertainty over future inflation or mortgage rate volatility. The household can benefit from the initial lower interest rate. If rates decline, the household's mortgage rate will decline without having to refinance. Sometimes personal circumstances can make ARMs attractive. For example, an ARM with a low rate that is locked for five years could be attractive to a household planning to move in four years.

In recent years in the United States, the delinquency rate on ARMs has usually been higher than the rate on similar FRMs.[41]

Shared-appreciation mortgages (SAMs) offer a reduced interest rate in return for a share of the appreciation of the house value.[42] Recently, there has been congressional interest in encouraging lenders to offer SAMs in return for principal writedowns for homeowners who owe more than their homes are worth (the so-called underwater houses). One issue with these mortgages is that it is not clear how improvements are reflected in the profit sharing. The sharing may also reduce the homeowner's financial incentive to maintain the property. On the other hand, shared appreciation offers lenders a hedge against inflation and lower interest rates for the borrower.

In any case, SAMs have never been very popular. Neither Fannie Mae nor Freddie Mac currently purchases SAMs. It appears that to purchase SAMs, Fannie Mae or Freddie Mac would have to request new program approval from FHFA, which has not approved the purchase of any new types of mortgages since the GSEs entered conservatorship. The Census Bureau does not publish statistics on the number of SAMs.

There have been proposals to have payments increase according to a standard schedule (the graduated payment mortgage) or to have payments vary according to the rate of inflation (the price level adjusted mortgage).

DETAILED TRENDS IN FUNDING RESIDENTIAL MORTGAGES

In looking broadly at more than 100 years of data on mortgage funding, there have been many changes in funding sources. Arguably, some of these changes were directly due to external forces such as federal legislation limiting or increasing the ability of banks to make mortgages; other changes were the result of lenders identifying profit opportunities. For more than 100 years, some financial entities have specialized in the originate-to-distribute (OTD) model: they lend money to homeowners and subsequently sell the mortgage to investors such as other banks. This sale can be done as a whole mortgage or as a part of a securitization, such as an MBS.

Economic historians have traced mortgage securitization to 1870 at least.[43] There are limited mortgage securitization data prior to 1952, and none of them are consistent with more modern data. Financial markets (including the mortgage market) continuously evolve, making comparisons of these markets over long periods more difficult.[44] Between 1900 and 1952, financial institutions[45] increased their share of direct funding of residential mortgages from slightly less than 50% to nearly 85%.[46] During this period, the average loan term ranged from 1.8 years (1921, commercial banks) to 22.1 years (1944, life insurance companies).[47]

> Over time, the OTD model evolved. In the 1950s, mortgage companies typically sold their loans to insurance companies, which kept them on portfolio as whole loans. Starting in the 1970s, this framework gave way to mortgage-backed securities (MBS), which were largely guaranteed by Ginnie Mae. The other government-sponsored housing agencies, Fannie Mae and Freddie Mac, became dominant players in the early 1980s. This period also saw the emergence of the private-label securities market, and in the 2000s, the private-label market grew at the expense of the agency market. However, the institutional framework of the OTD model remained more or less identical to what it was in the 1950s. Lenders originated loans and sold them to other institutions. Typically the loans were then serviced by the originating lender, but other servicing arrangements were also possible.[48]

Since 1952, the Federal Reserve has provided data on direct sources of funds as well as the indirect sources of funds that are channeled through securitization (**Figure 3**). The securitization data include only GSE and government agency MBSs. In 1952, the major sources of direct funding of mortgages were commercial banks, households lending to each other, savings institutions such as savings and loans, and life insurance companies. Direct sources of funds increased in current dollars from $59 billion in 1952 to $10.3 trillion in 2011. U.S.-chartered commercial banks increased their holdings of mortgages from $10 billion in 1952 to $2.1 trillion.

Figure 3 has been arranged to show insured depositories (commercial banks and savings institutions) at the bottom of the graph. Their combined shares reached a maximum of 75% of direct funding in 1973, and they provided over 50% of direct funding between 1952 and 1985. Starting in 1952, households and nonprofits became less important over time, but did provide about 5% each year between 1980 and 1988, as did life insurance companies.

Savings institutions, including savings and loans, lost market share after 1978. The first signs of the savings and loan crisis occurred in 1984-1986.[49] Resolving failed savings and loans continued until the mid-1990s.[50]

Meanwhile, the GSEs first provided 5% or more of direct funding in 1970 and in general their market share grew until recently. Between 2005 and 2009, the GSEs' market share fell below 50%, but since 2009 their share has been greater than 50%. Since the mid-1990s, PLS (private-label securitizations, also called issuers of asset-backed securities by the Fed) have been significant, but much smaller than the GSEs and government agencies.

Commercial banks have supplied 10%-20% of direct funding over the 1952-2011 time period.

Figure 4 summarizes Federal Reserve data showing who holds 5% or more of the outstanding bonds, and MBSs of government and GSEs. The MBSs are backed by single- and multifamily housing, farm homes, and commercial real estate. Single-family homes represent most of the MBSs, but they are not separated out by the Fed.

The current dollar value of the securities grew from $2.2 billion in 1952[51] to $7.6 trillion at the end of 2011, so while the market share for U.S.-chartered commercial banks declined from 76% to 19%, their holdings increased from $1.7 billion[52] to $1.415 trillion.

In 1952, the major holders of mortgage securities were state and local governments (22%) and U.S.-chartered commercial banks (76%). In 2011, major holders of these mortgage securities included foreigners (rest of world, 14%), the Fed (monetary authority, 12%), U.S.-chartered commercial banks (19%), and mutual funds (13%). The "other" category grew from 3% in 1952 to 32% in 2011. Looking over the 60 years of data in 10-year intervals, only commercial banks have been consistently important.

The rest of the world had become major holders by 2001. GSEs were major holders 1996-2009. State and local governments were important until 1991. Savings institutions (such as savings and loans) were important 1957-1991.

Additional research could analyze why each of these financial sectors became important and then lost importance, but these data suggest that the sources of funding mortgages has fluctuated over the past 60 years. Given this history, it seems likely even without the 2008 financial crisis, funding sources would continue to change over the next 60 years.

Growth of Securitization

Since Ginnie Mae issued the first residential MBSs in 1970, loan securitization has replaced deposits to fund commercial mortgages, small business loans, automobile loans, credit card debt, student loans, and loans that qualify for Community Reinvestment Act (P.L. 95-128) credit.[53] These non-mortgage securitizations have become known as asset-backed securitizations (ABSs).

Like MBS proceeds, the proceeds from selling the ABSs can be used to fund loans, which are packaged into additional ABSs. Servicing the underlying loans can remain with the original lender or can be sold. When the original lender retains the servicing rights, the borrower has no indication who owns the loan.

The main advantages to consumers of securitization come from indirect access to the world's financial markets: more available credit and lower interest rates. The main disadvantages are the possibilities that not everyone's incentives are aligned, and the cost of securitization.

Securitization enables lenders to make more loans than their balance sheets would otherwise justify if the loans were retained. Many lenders have found the "originate-to-distribute" model more profitable than the "originate-to-hold" model.

Originators earn fees from creating the loan; they can make a profit selling the loan; they can earn fees from servicing the loan; and because the loan is no longer on their balance sheet, they have reduced their capital requirements. The efficiency of the originate-to-distribute model depends on the originators accurately characterizing the risk and return of the assets.

1952-2011

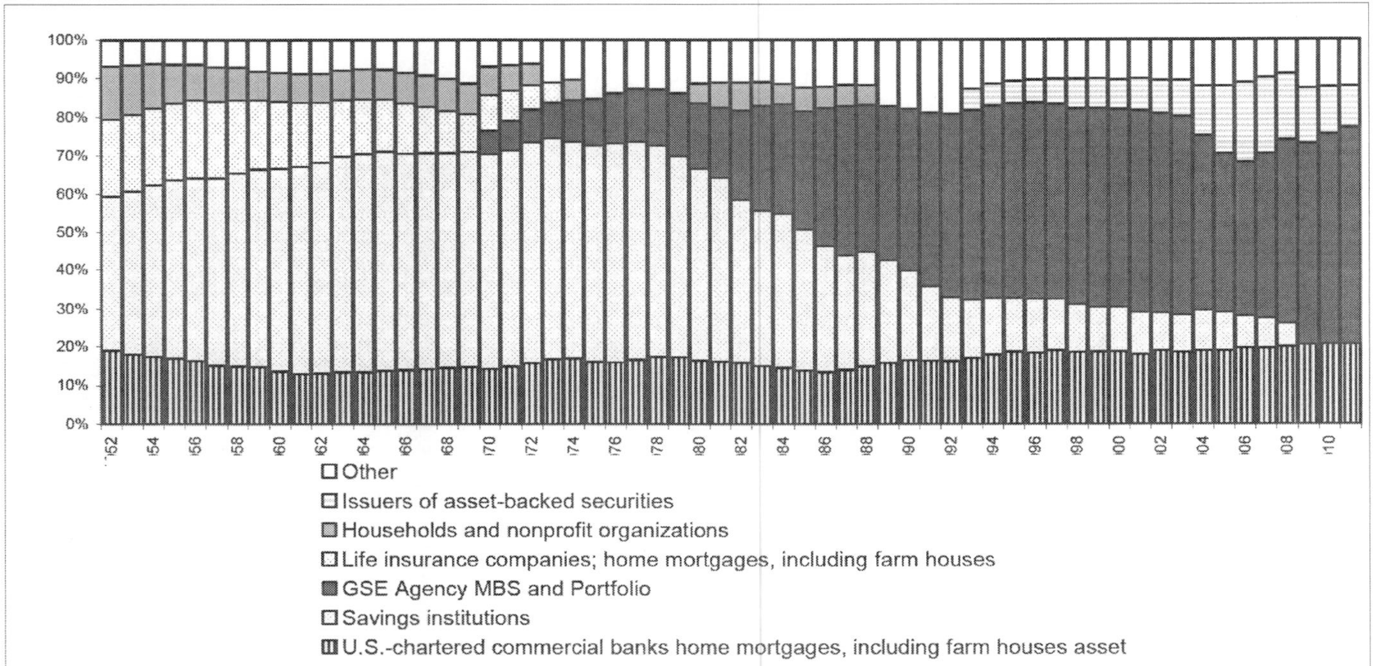

Source: Federal Reserve, "Table L. 218, Home Mortgages," *Flow of Funds: Historical Data*, March 8, 2012, available at http://www.federalreserve.gov/releases/z1/ and CRScalculations.

Note: Sources with a market share of 5% or less are included in the other category.

Figure 3. Major Direct Sources of Residential Mortgage Funds.

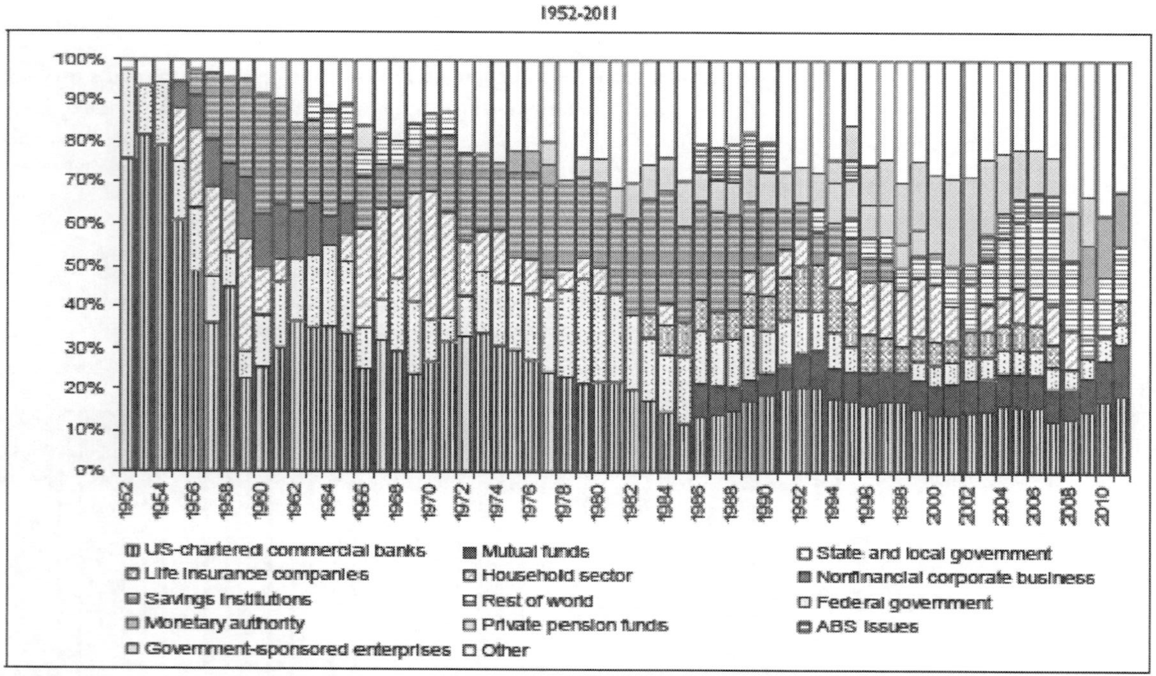

Source: Federal Reserve, "Table L. 210, Agency – and GSE-backed Securities," *Flow of Funds: Historical Data*, March 8, 2012, available at http://www.federalreserve. gov/releases/z1/ and CRS Calculations.

Notes: Includes bonds and MBSs for government agencies and GSEs. MBSs securitize single family residences, multifamily housing, commercial real estate and farm housing. Sources with a market share of 5% or less are included in the other category.

Figure 4. Major Holders of Mortgage-Backed Securities.

ABSs must conform to various securities laws and regulations, and compliance can be costly. As a result, ABS issues are typically for millions or even billions of dollars, and each issue is sold to many institutional investors. These investors are not experts in making, underwriting, or servicing the underlying loans. Instead, the investors depend on specialists. The underwriting (credit evaluation) is sometimes supplemented by securing additional guarantees to reduce the investor's exposure to credit risk.

In the area of securitization, Fannie Mae's and Freddie Mac's charters provide three competitive advantages compared to private-label securitizers. First, they are exempt from the requirement that they register all their securities with the SEC.[54] This makes issuing MBSs less expensive, and it allows them to lock mortgage rates before mortgages are closed.[55] Second, even before the GSEs were placed in conservatorship, it was widely perceived that the federal government implicitly guaranteed their MBSs. Third, the relatively small capital requirements in their charters allowed Fannie Mae and Freddie Mac to charge less for a better guarantee than non-GSE competitors could offer.

Many lenders "swap" their mortgages with Fannie or Freddie for MBSs backed exclusively by those mortgages which the lender originated. Lenders pay the GSEs a guarantee fee for the transaction. In return, the lenders have the mortgages that they know because they originated them, can sell the MBSs if desired, and carry no credit risk.

One result of these features is that there is a liquid market for many ABSs and MBSs, which means that investors are able to buy and sell these securities quickly with little effect on price. An institution can purchase MBSs backed by 30-year fixed rate mortgages and sell the MBSs at the market price at any time in the future. Both Fannie Mae and Freddie Mac maintain active trading desks to enhance the liquidity of their MBSs.[56] This liquidity further reduces the interest rate sought by investors.

The FHA/Ginnie Mae combination places the credit risk with the U.S. government by providing the full faith and credit of the federal government as a guarantee of timely payment.

Private label securitizations use the ratings of the nationally recognized statistical ratings organizations (NRSROs), such as Moody's, Standard & Poor's, and Fitch, as third party due diligence and assurance that the underlying loans are sound. Private label ABSs can use additional credit enhancement techniques such as third party guarantees (financial backing by independent companies that charge a fee for the service), over-collateralizations (pledging more collateral than the value of the security), and letters of credit (commitments to loan funds to the issuer of the security) to reduce the risk to the investor and thereby reduce the interest rate required by the investor.

In summary, government-related MBSs have been a model for the securitization of other types of consumer loans. MBSs have broadened the source of funding and made mortgages more available than they would be without international institutional investors. The private sector has devoted more funding to ABSs, which Fannie Mae, Freddie Mac, and Ginnie Mae do not issue.

APPENDIX A. GOVERNMENT SUPPORT OF HOMEOWNERSHIP

This appendix draws on previous research to list government programs that support homeownership, after which it provides a summary of the major policy arguments in favor and against these programs.[57]

Government Programs

Federal, state, and local governments intervene to support housing markets in a number of ways. Interest on most home mortgages is deductible from federal and most state individual income taxes for homeowners who itemize deductions. Individuals who itemize can also deduct state and local property taxes paid on homes. The government has created Fannie Mae, Freddie Mac, the Federal Home Loan Bank System, FHA, Ginnie Mae, USDA Rural Housing, and the Department of Veterans' Affairs to encourage homeownership by providing guarantees to reduce the risk to lenders and expand mortgage lending.

The Housing Inspectors General (IGs of HUD, U.S. Department of Agriculture, U.S. Department of Veterans' Affairs, and FHFA) have compiled a report summarizing the federal government's single-family mortgage programs. The Housing IGs list the following HUD programs:

- One- to Four-Family Home Mortgage Insurance
- Single Family Disposition Program
- Mortgage Insurance for Disaster Victims

- Rehabilitation Loan Insurance
- Energy Efficient Mortgage Insurance
- Good Neighbor Next Door
- Graduated Payment Mortgage
- FHA Home Affordable Modification Program (HAMP)
- Loss Mitigation
- Manufactured Homes Loan Insurance (Title I)
- Property Improvement Loan Insurance (Title I)
- Home Equity Conversion Mortgage
- HOPE for Homeowners
- Insured Mortgages on Hawaiian Home Lands
- FHA Insured Mortgages on Indian Land
- Neighborhood Stabilization Program 1
- Neighborhood Stabilization Program 2
- Neighborhood Stabilization Program 3
- Emergency Homeowners' Loan Program
- Ginnie Mae Mortgage-Backed Securities (MBSs)

The Housing IGs list two USDA programs:

- Single Family Housing Guaranteed Loan Program (GLP)
- Single Family Housing Direct Loan Program (DLP)

They list one VA program:

- VA Home Loan Program

At FHFA, they list programs run by Fannie Mae, Freddie Mac, and the Federal Home Loan Banks:

- Making Home Affordable Programs
- Mortgage-Backed Securities Program
- Mortgage Purchasing and Retained Portfolio
- Mortgage Servicing Program
- Real Estate Owned Purchasing and Financing Program
- Acquired Member Asset (AMA) Program
- Advances, Letters of Credit, and Lines of Credit

- Affordable Housing Program (AHP) and Community Investment Program (CIP)
- Office of Finance Debt Issuance
- Private-Label Mortgage Purchases Program

Provisions in the tax code that reduce the tax liabilities of individual income taxpayers for activities related to homeownership include the following:[58]

- Deduction for Mortgage Interest on Owner-Occupied Residences
- Deduction for Property Taxes on Owner-Occupied Residences
- Increased Standard Deduction of Real Property Taxes on Owner-Occupied Residences[59]
- Deduction for Premiums for Qualified Mortgage Insurance
- Exclusion of Capital Gains on Sales of Principal Residences
- Exclusion of Interest on State and Local Government Bonds for Owner-Occupied Housing
- First-Time Homebuyer Tax Credit
- Exclusion of Income Attributable to the Discharge of Principal Residence Acquisition Indebtedness

Policy Reasons Advanced for and against Government Support

Economists and policy analysts usually begin their analysis of proposed or actual government interventions by asking, "What is the market failure?" In other words, what prevents competition in the marketplace from delivering the desired amount of a good or service in the most efficient manner with the lowest price?

Local governments intervene with building codes and inspections to increase information and standardization with local building codes inspections to prevent hiding information about defects and substandard construction techniques.

Some supporters of government programs that promote homeownership argue that homeownership benefits society in general, not just the specific homeowner. In economic terms, owner-occupied housing is argued to generate positive externalities. According to this analysis, unless there is some way for the homeowner to capture the externalities, the homeowner will buy less housing. One way to correct for the externalities and to encourage the optimal level of owner-occupied housing is to subsidize homeownership. In the United States, tax deductions can accomplish this.

Research has found that compared to otherwise identical renters, homeowners have more political knowledge, are more active politically, maintain their homes better, and have children who do better in school.[60] On the other hand, correlations do not prove causation, and individuals who are politically active and motivated to maintain their residence are more likely to become homeowners. There could be other unobserved factors at work here.

Another argument in favor of support for homeownership is that this subsidization balances the subsidies provided for renting, such as Section 8 vouchers.[61] Counterarguments to this include that subsidies to rental housing could be cut and that the rental subsidies go mostly to lower-income households and the homeownership subsidies to middle- and upper-income households.

Robert J. Shiller has argued that encouraging homeownership "has a great deal to do with culture, and little to do with financial wisdom."[62] He also has argued that homeownership results in households having investment portfolios that contain relatively too much exposure to real estate relative to other assets and are not diversified.

Peter J. Wallison, co-director of the American Enterprise Institute's program on financial policy studies, has identified, and rejected, four other reasons for government support of housing finance.[63] First, he examines whether government backing is necessary to have a 30-year fixed-rate mortgage, and he points to the jumbo mortgage market as proof that this is not necessary.

Second, he suggests that government support might be necessary to keep a steady flow of funds to home building, but notes that other industries survive without such government backing.

Third, he proposes and rejects the idea that investors require a federal guarantee if they are to purchase mortgages or MBSs. He argues that current investors such as central banks, U.S.-chartered commercial banks, savings and loans, and government pension plans value safety very highly when making investment decisions; they would be replaced by other institutional investors if mortgage underwriting were sound and mortgage rates higher.

In addition, he argues that even if there is a policy purpose to subsidizing homeownership for low-income households, it should be more narrowly targeted.

APPENDIX B. A BRIEF HISTORY OF GOVERNMENT-SPONSORED ENTERPRISES AND HOUSING

In 1932, the FHLBanks were created to provide direct support to savings and loan associations and savings banks, which in turn supported the mortgage market. In 1938, Fannie Mae was created to provide mortgage liquidity to lenders. In 1970, Freddie Mac was created as a part of the Federal Home Loan Bank System to compete with Fannie Mae and to provide liquidity to savings and loan associations and to savings banks, which at the time were important mortgage lenders. At the time, interstate banking was prohibited, encouraging the existence of many local financial markets instead of one national market.

The Federal Home Loan Banks (FHLBanks)

The Federal Home Loan Bank Act of 1932 created the FHLBank System as "mixed-ownership government corporations."[64] The intent was to increase mortgage availability during banking contractions and to provide a source of funds for members to use to smooth over deposit withdrawals or to respond to mortgage applications and renewals beyond what their deposits would allow. Savings and loan associations were required to become members and to purchase non-public stock of the appropriate regional bank.[65] The regional banks made loans (called "advances") secured by mortgages to members. Initially, advances were limited to homes worth no more than $20,000; presently the nationwide limit is $417,000 (and up to $625,500 in high-cost areas).[66]

The act provided for the establishment of 8 to 12 regional banks (similar to the Federal Reserve's regional banks), to enhance the mortgage industry's liquidity. The FHLBanks obtained the money that they lent to their members by selling non-public stock to the Treasury and to their members, and by selling bonds to the public. The 12 FHLBanks redeemed the Treasury's stock by 1951, making the banks privately owned by the FHLBank members.

Each regional bank is federally chartered with its own board of directors. System members are subject to Federal Home Loan Bank Board regulation. The FHLBanks are jointly and severally liable for each others' debt, leading some observers to call the banks a collective or cooperative GSE.

Initially oversight of the FHLBanks was vested in a board of five directors appointed by the President with Senate confirmation.[67] In later years, minor changes were made to the structure of the FHLBank Board, including changing its name to the Federal Housing Finance Board, which the Housing and Economic Recovery Act of 2008 (HERA, P.L. 110-289) replaced with the Federal Housing Finance Agency (FHFA) in 2008.

Federal National Mortgage Association (Fannie Mae)

Fannie Mae traces its creation to the 1935 RFC (Reconstruction Finance Corporation) Mortgage Company, which authorized the chartering of companies to purchase existing home mortgages.[68] There were no private sector applications, and in 1938, the Federal Housing Administration (FHA) chartered the National Mortgage Association as a subsidiary of the RFC Mortgage Company to create a market to buy FHA-insured mortgages. Later that year the National Mortgage Association changed its name to the Federal National Mortgage Association, which still is Fannie Mae's legal name.[69] When Fannie Mae was created, the maximum mortgage size that it could purchase was $16,000.

Originally, Fannie Mae provided subsidized mortgages (called special housing assistance) for government programs and purchased only FHA-insured mortgages, but in 1946 it was authorized to purchase Veterans Administration (VA)-guaranteed mortgages. Until 1981, Fannie Mae held its mortgage purchases in portfolio and financed its purchases by selling bonds.

In 1946, Fannie Mae obtained additional financing to purchase more mortgages by selling preferred stock to the Treasury.[70] In 1954, Fannie Mae sold non-voting common stock to those selling it mortgages and purchased additional mortgages.[71]

In 1950, Fannie Mae was transferred to the Housing and Home Finance Agency (HHFA).

In 1965, HHFA (including Fannie Mae) became part of the newly created Department of Housing and Urban Development (HUD). While part of HUD, Fannie Mae's board of directors consisted of the Secretary of HUD as chair and four other government employees. In addition, Congress or the President could ask Fannie Mae to provide "special assistance" in the mortgage market in the form of subsidized housing, and the management and liquidation of certain mortgages.

The Housing and Urban Development Act of 1968 (P.L. 90-448) divided Fannie Mae into two parts: (1) a government corporation, the Government National Mortgage Association or Ginnie Mae, and (2) a GSE, Fannie Mae.[72]

Ginnie Mae assumed the special housing assistance functions and the management functions of the old Fannie Mae. The new Fannie Mae was to provide access to the secondary mortgage market for FHA and VA mortgages. The federal government sold its Fannie Mae shares, and Fannie Mae sold additional shares to the public.

In 1970, when Freddie Mac was created to deal in conventional mortgages, Fannie Mae was authorized to purchase conventional loans on moderate-income housing. Also in 1970, Ginnie Mae began to guarantee FHA/VA mortgage-backed securities.

Fannie Mae's stock traded on the NYSE with the symbol FNM until June 16, 2010, when FHFA ordered them to be delisted rather than attempt to continue to meet the NYSE's $1.00 minimum share price rule. Fannie Mae now trades over-the-counter with the symbol FNMA.[73]

Federal Home Loan Mortgage Corporation (Freddie Mac)

In 1970, Congress chartered Freddie Mac as part of the FHLBank System to provide competition to Fannie Mae and to provide additional liquidity for conventional mortgages. Freddie Mac was to provide access to the secondary mortgage market for FHLBank System members.

Freddie Mac raised its initial capital by selling stock to the regional FHLBanks.

In 1971, Freddie Mac followed Ginnie Mae's lead and offered its first mortgage-backed security (MBS), which Freddie Mac called a Participation Certificate (PC). These MBSs, which pool mortgages into large securities, direct funds from institutional investors to the U.S. mortgage market. Freddie Mac gave FHLBank members the option of either selling mortgages to its regional FHLBank, which would sell them to Freddie Mac, or using the mortgage as collateral for an advance.

Freddie Mac would pool the mortgages into an MBS, guarantee that investors would receive timely payment of principal and interest, sell the MBS to an investor, and use the proceeds to purchase additional mortgages. The regional FHLBank could purchase more mortgages from members, who could in turn make more mortgages.

From its creation until the Financial Institutions Reform, Recovery, and Enforcement Act of 1989 (FIRREA)[74] made it stockholder owned in 1990, Freddie Mac's board of directors had the same three members as the FHLBank Board's. Freddie Mac's stock traded on the New York Stock Exchange

(NYSE) with the symbol FRE until June 16, 2010, when FHFA ordered them to be delisted rather than attempt to continue to meet the NYSE's $1.00 minimum share price rule. Freddie Mac now trades over-the-counter with the symbol FMCC.[75]

Government Oversight

At their start, Fannie Mae and the FHLBanks were subject to government oversight as federal agencies. When they first became GSEs, Fannie Mae (1977) and Freddie Mac (1988) were overseen by the Department of Housing and Urban Development (HUD). The Federal Home Loan Bank Act of 1932 created the Federal Home Loan Bank Board to oversee the FHLBanks. Savings and loans and savings banks became members of the Federal Home Loan Bank System, and the board regulated the savings and loan industry, including Freddie Mac.

In part in response to the savings and loan crisis, the Financial Institutions Reform, Recovery, and Enforcement Act of 1989 (FIRREA, P.L. 101-73) separated Freddie Mac from the FHLBank system and made it a publicly traded company with HUD as its regulator. FIRREA create the Federal Housing Finance Board as a replacement for Federal Home Loan Bank Board to oversee the FHLBanks. The Office of Thrift Supervision (OTS) took over regulation of savings and loan associations.

The Federal Housing Enterprises Financial Safety and Soundness Act of 1992 (FHEFSSA, P.L. 102-550) created OFHEO as an independent agency within HUD as the safety and soundness regulator for Fannie Mae and Freddie Mac. OFHEO was authorized to set capital requirements, conduct annual risk-based examinations, and generally enforce compliance with safety and soundness standards to make sure that Fannie Mae and Freddie Mac did not take advantage of their implicit guarantees by increasing profits by taking excessive risks. OFHEO was generally considered a weak regulator, in part because it was funded by appropriations instead of assessments on Fannie Mae and Freddie Mac.

HUD itself was assigned the task of setting housing goals for central cities, rural areas, and other underserved areas, low- and moderate-income census tracts, minority census tracts, low- and moderate income, and special affordable housing goals for Fannie Mae and Freddie Mac.

The Housing and Economic Recovery Act of 2008 (HERA, P.L. 110-289) consolidated all regulatory oversight of Fannie Mae, Freddie Mac, and the

Federal Home Loan Banks in the Federal Housing Finance Agency, which is independent of other agencies. In September 2008, Fannie Mae and Freddie Mac agreed to be placed in conservatorship under FHFA. This means that FHFA has the right to run the two GSEs.

End Notes

[1] The Federal Home Loan Banks form a third collective housing GSE and Ginnie Mae (officially, the Government National Mortgage Association) is a government agency and part of the Department of Housing and Urban Development. Neither would be directly affected by the legislation discussed in this report, and they are discussed only in passing. Reflecting congressional emphasis on Fannie Mae and Freddie Mac, this report uses the term GSEs to refer to Fannie Mae and Freddie Mac, not the Federal Home Loan Banks or Ginnie Mae.

[2] U.S. Federal Housing Finance Agency, *Enterprise Share of Residential Mortgage Debt Outstanding 1990 - 2010 (XLS file)*, available at http://www.fhfa.gov/Default.aspx?Page=70. FHFA has not released more recent data.

[3] See CRS Report R40800, *GSEs and the Government's Role in Housing Finance: Issues for the 112th Congress*, by N. Eric Weiss; CRS Report R41719, *The Obama Administration's Report on "Reforming America's Housing Finance Market": Implications for Fannie Mae and Freddie Mac*, by N. Eric Weiss; and Board of Governors, Federal Reserve System, *The U.S. Housing Market: Current Conditions and Policy Considerations*, January 4, 2012, available at http://federalreserve.gov/publications/other-reports/files/housing-white-paper-20120104.pdf.

[4] CRS Report R41822, *Proposals to Reform Fannie Mae and Freddie Mac in the 112th Congress*, by N. Eric Weiss.

[5] For more information on covered bonds, see CRS Report RS22925, *Covered Bonds: An Alternative to Securitization for Funding Mortgages*, by Edward V. Murphy and CRS Report R41322, *Covered Bonds: Issues in the 112th Congress*, by Edward V. Murphy. The House Financial Services Committee reported the bill as amended on March 5, 2012.

[6] National Commission on Fiscal Responsibility and Reform, *The Moment of Truth: Report of the National Commission on Fiscal Responsibility and Reform*, December 2010, p. 31, http://www.fiscalcommission.gov/sites/fiscalcommission.gov/files/documents/TheMomentofTruth12_1_2010.pdf.

[7] CRS Report R41596, *The Mortgage Interest and Property Tax Deductions: Analysis and Options*, by Mark P. Keightley, p. 14-19.

[8] CRS Report RS22172, *The Conforming Loan Limit*, by N. Eric Weiss and Sean M. Hoskins.

[9] U.S. Department of Treasury, and U.S. Department of Housing and Urban Development, *Reforming America's Housing Finance Market: A Report to Congress*, February 2011, http://portal.hud.gov/hudportal/documents/huddoc?id=housingfinmarketreform.pdf.

[10] CRS Report R41958, *Upcoming Rules Pursuant to the Dodd-Frank Act: Spring 2011 Unified Agenda*, by Maeve P. Carey and Curtis W. Copeland.

[11] CRS Report R42056, *Ability to Repay, Risk-Retention Standards, and Mortgage Credit Access*, by Darryl E. Getter and U.S. Federal Housing Finance Agency, *Qualified Residential Mortgages*, Mortgage Market Note 11-02, April 11,2011, available at http://www.fhfa.gov/webfiles/20686/QRM_FINAL_ALL_R41111.pdf.

[12] Federal Reserve System, "Regulation Z; Truth in Lending," 76 *Federal Register* 27930-27506, May 11, 2011.

[13] U.S. Consumer Financial Protection Bureau, *Examination Report,* available at http://www.consumerfinance.gov/wp-content/themes/cfpb_theme/supervision-manual/PartIIICFPB

supervisionmanual.pdf. See, also, Ashley Gordon, U.S. CFPB, "What the Proposed Mortgage Servicing Rules Could Mean for You," April 10, 2012, http://www.consumer finance.gov/blog/what-the-proposed-mortgage-servicing-rules-could-mean-for-you/.

[14] U.S. Federal Deposit Insurance Corporation, "Risk-Based Capital Guidelines; Capital Adequacy Guidelines; Capital Maintenance; Capital-Residential Mortgage Loans Modified Pursuant to the Home Affordable Mortgage Program," 74 *Federal Register* 60137, November 20, 2009.

[15] Covered bonds are an alternative to MBS for raising large amounts of money to fund mortgages. For more details, see CRS Report R41322, *Covered Bonds: Issues in the 112th Congress*, by Edward V. Murphy. Also, Federal Deposit Insurance Corporation, "Covered Bond Policy Statement," 73 *Federal Register* 43754, July 28, 2008.

[16] Board of Governors of the Federal Reserve System, *The U.S. Housing Market: Current Conditions and Policy Considerations*, Jan. 4, 2012, available at http://federalreserve.gov/ publications/other-reports/files/housing-white-paper-20120104.pdf.

[17] The homeownership rate is the percentage of households that own their homes. This includes homes owned subject to a mortgage.

[18] People occupying a room without cooking facilities are not considered to be a household.

[19] Carlos Garriga, William T. Gavin, and Don Schlagenhauf, "Recent Trends in Homeownership," *Federal Reserve of St. Louis Review*, September/October 2006, pp. 397-412. http://research.stlouisfed.org/publications/review/06/09/ Garriga.pdf, also Mark Doms and Meryl Motika, "The Rise in Homeownership," *FRBSF Economic Letter,* Number 2006-30, November 2006, http://www.frbsf.org/publications/economics/letter/2006/el2006-30.pdf

[20] Board of Governors of the Federal Reserve, *Senior Loan Officer Opinion Survey on Bank Lending Practices*, April 2012, pp. 33-49, http://www.federalreserve.gov/boarddocs/ snloansurvey/201205/fullreport.pdf and Kate Berry, "Capital One Still Not Accepting FHA Loans with Low Credit Scores," *American Banker On Line*, February 16, 2012.

[21] Arguably, renters benefit from the ability of owners of rental property to deduct the costs of operating the property, including interest on mortgages and taxes.

[22] Officially, Ginnie Mae is the Government National Mortgage Association.

[23] Officially, Fannie Mae is the Federal National Mortgage Association, and Freddie Mac is the Federal Home Loan Mortgage Corporation.

[24] CRS Report RS22172, *The Conforming Loan Limit*, by N. Eric Weiss and Sean M. Hoskins.

[25] A third housing GSE, the Federal Home Loan Bank System, makes loans backed by eligible collateral (primarily mortgages) to member depositories. For more information on the system, see CRS Report RL32815, *Federal Home Loan Bank System: Policy Issues*, by Edward V. Murphy.

[26] Al Yoon, "Rare Residential Mortgage Bond Tests Dormant Market," *The Wall Street Journal*, January 12, 2012, On Line, WSJ Blogs, Developments, http://blogs.wsj.com/developments/ 2012/01/12/rare-residential-mortgage-bond-tests-dormant-market/.

[27] U.S. Federal Housing Finance Agency, *Data as of May 10, 2012 on Treasury and Federal Reserve Purchase Programs for GSE and Mortgage-Related Securities*. This is updated quarterly and a link to the latest version is available at http://www.fhfa.gov/Default.aspx? Page=70.

[28] U.S. Treasury, "Chart of the Day: Treasury Completes MBS Portfolio Wind Down, Generates $25 Billion Positive Return for Taxpayers," press release, March 19, 2012, http://www. treasury.gov/connect/blog/Pages/Chart-of-the-Day-Treasury-Completes-MBS-Portfolio-Wind-Down-Generates-25-Billion-Positive-Return-for-Taxpayers.aspx.

[29] U.S. Congress, House Committee on Financial Services, Subcommittee on Oversight and Investigations, *Oversight of the Federal Housing Finance Agency*, 112th Cong., 1st sess., December 1, 2011.

[30] U.S. Congress, Senate Committee on Banking, Housing, and Urban Affairs, Subcommittee on Housing, Transportation and Community Development, *Strengthening the Housing Market and Minimizing Losses to Taxpayers*, 112th Cong., 2nd sess., March 15, 2012.

[31] U.S. House of Representatives, Committee on Financial Services, Hearing entitled "Perspectives on the Health of the FHA Single-family Insurance Fund," Dec. 1, 2011. Testimony and archived webcast of the hearing are available at http://financialservices. house.gov/Calendar/EventSingle.aspx?EventID=270311.

[32] Census Bureau, "Historical Census of Housing Tables: Homeownership," press release, http:// www.census.gov/hhes/www/housing/census/historic/owner.html.

[33] James Poterba and Todd Sinai, "Tax Expenditures for Owner-Occupied Housing: Deductions for Property Taxes and Mortgage Interest and the Exclusion of Imputed Rental Income," *American Economic Review*, vol. 98, no. 2 (May2008), pp. 84-89.

[34] Between the end of the Depression and the current housing market decline, some state and regional house prices declined, including farm and industrial states (early 1980s), energy states (mid-1980s). See David C. Wheelock, "What Happens to Banks When House Prices Fall? U.S. Regional Housing Busts of the 1980s and 1990s," *Federal Reserve Bank of St. Louis Review*, September/October 2006, 88(5), pp. 413-29. For more collected data on house price declines see Federal Reserve Bank of New York, *Synopses of Selected Research on Housing, Mortgages, and Foreclosures*, Sept. 1, 2008, http://www.newyorkfed.org/ regional/Synopses.pdf.

[35] Data are reported annually between 1891 and 1952, and quarterly since 1953. The changes in this discussion are annual (i.e., quarterly data is analyzed compared to the same quarter a year earlier).

[36] U.S. Census Bureau, "Table 3-15, Mortgage Characteristics," *American Housing Survey: 2009*, available at http://www.census.gov/housing/ahs/data/ahs2009.html and CRS calculations.

[37] P.L. 97-320, Title VIII, Alternative Mortgage Transactions Parity Act of 1982.

[38] An ARM is sometimes identified differently than a fixed-rate mortgage (FRM). For example, a five year ARM usually is a 30-year mortgage with a fixed rate for the first five years and adjustable rates for the remaining life of the loan.

[39] U.S. Census Bureau, *op. cit.*

[40] For example, James Vickery, "Interest Rates and Consumer Choice in the Residential Mortgage Market," presented at the American Economic Association Meetings, January 2007, available at http://www.aeaweb.org/annual_mtg_papers/2007/0105_1430_0102.pdf.

[41] See Freddie Mac, "Monthly Volume Summaries," http://www.freddiemac.com/investors/ volsum/, Fannie Mae, "Monthly Summary," http://www.fanniemae.com/portal/about-us/ investor-relations/monthly-summary.html, and Mortgage Bankers Association, "MBA's Quarterly National Delinquency Survey," http://www.mortgagebankers.org/ ResearchandForecasts/ProductsandSurveys/NationalDelinquencySurvey.htm.

[42] Daniel J. Larkins, "Recent Developments in Mortgage Markets," *Survey of Current Business*, vol. 62, no. 2 (February 1982), pp. 19-36, http://www.bea.gov/scb/pdf/1982/0282cont.pdf.

[43] Kenneth A. Snowden, "Mortgage Securitization in the United States: Twentieth Century Developments in Historical Perspective," in *Anglo-American Financial Systems: Institutions and Markets in the Twentieth Century*, ed. Michael D. Bordo and Richard Sylla (New York: Irwin, 1955), pp. 261-298.

[44] One source of data and analysis of earlier mortgage4 financing sources is Leo Grebler, David M. Blank, and Louis Winnick, *Capital Formation in Residential Real Estate: Trends and Prospects,* (Princeton, NJ: Princeton University Press, 1956), pp. 190-208.

[45] This is drawn from Grebler, Bland, and Winnick, who define financial institutions to include commercial banks, mutual savings banks, savings and loans, life insurance companies, other insurance companies, mortgage companies, installment investment companies and two government agencies: the Home Owners' Loan Corporation (now defunct), and the Federal National Mortgage Association (at the time a government agency).

[46] Grebler, Bland, and Winnick.

[47] J. E. Morton, *Urban Mortgage Lending: Comparative Markets and Experience* (Princeton University Press, 1956), pp. 174-175, http://www.nber.org/books/mort56-1.

[48] Christopher L. Foote, Kristopher S. Gerardi, and Kristopher S. Gerardi, *Why Did So Many People Make So Many Ex Post Bad Decisions? The Causes of the Foreclosure Crisis*, Federal Reserve Bank of Boston, Public Policy Discussion Pater, No. 12-2, May 2, 2012, p. 23, http://www.bostonfed.org/economic/ppdp/2012/ppdp1202.pdf.

[49] Federal Deposit Insurance Corporation, *The S&L Crisis: A Chrono-Bibliography*, http://www.fdic.gov/bank/historical/s%26l/.

[50] Timothy Curry and Lynn Shibut, "The Cost of the Savings and Loan Crisis: Truth and Consequences," *FDIC Banking Review*, 2000, pp. 26-35, http://fcx.fdic.gov/bank/analytical/banking/2000dec/brv13n2_2.pdf.

[51] $19.0 billion in 2011 dollars according to the Bureau of Labor Statistic's Consumer Price Index calculator at http://bls.gov/data/inflation_calculator.htm.

[52] $14.3 billion in 2011 dollars.

[53] The securitization of commercial real estate was common in the 1920s and some residential mortgages were pooled into guaranteed mortgage participation certificates issued by title and insurance companies. See William N. Goetzmann and Frank Newman, *Securitization in the 1920s*, National Bureau of Economic Research, Working Paper 15650, January 2010, http://www.nber.org/papers/w15650.

[54] Fannie Mae: 12 U.S.C. 1723c; Freddie Mac: 12 U.S.C. 1455(d).

[55] Non-GSEs must register their MBS with the SEC. This requires being able to identify the mortgages being securitized. Fannie Mae and Freddie Mac specify certain minimum standards for the mortgages that will be securitized and investors bid on the assumption that all of the mortgages will be at the minimum levels.

[56] This liquidity makes the MBS more valuable (and more profitable to the Enterprises), and the trading desks are profitable.

[57] Summaries of federal support for homeownership include U.S. Congressional Budget Office, *An Overview of Federal Support for Housing,* Nov. 3, 2009, http://www.cbo.gov/ftpdocs/105xx/doc10525/11-03-HousingPrograms.pdf. and U.S. Federal Housing Inspectors General, *Compendium of Federal Single Family Mortgage Programs and Related Activities*, November 2011, http://www.fhfaoig.gov/Content/Files/compendium.pdf.

[58] U.S. Congress, Senate Committee on the Budget, *Tax Expenditures: Compendium of Background Material on Individual Provisions*, committee print, prepared by Congressional Research Service, 111th Cong., 2nd sess., December 2010, S.Rept. 111-58 (Washington: GPO, 2010), pp. 335-374.

[59] Taxpayers that do not itemize and pay property taxes may take a deduction in addition to the standard deduction, ibid. p. 341.

[60] Two articles that summarize this research are N. Edward Coulson, "Housing Policy and the Social Benefits of Homeownership," *Federal Reserve Bank of Philadelphia, Business Review*, Second Quarter 2002, pp. 7-10, http://www.phil.frb.org/research-and-data/publications/business-review/2002/q2/brq202ec.pdf and William G. Gale, Jonathan Gruber, and Seth Stephens-Davidowitz, "Encouraging Homeownership Through the Tax Code," *Tax Notes*, June 18, 2007, pp. 1171-1189.

[61] For details on the Section 8 program, see CRS Report RL32284, *An Overview of the Section 8 Housing Programs: Housing Choice Vouchers and Project-Based Rental Assistance*, by Maggie McCarty. For information on rental assistance programs in general, see CRS Report RL34591, *Overview of Federal Housing Assistance Programs and Policy*, by Maggie McCarty et al.

[62] Robert J. Shiller, "Mom, Apple Pie and Mortgages," *New York Times*, March 7, 2010, Business Section, p. 8, Late Edition - Final.

[63] Peter J. Wallison, *A New Housing Finance System for the United States*, available at http://www.aei.org/files/2012/03/02/-a-new-housing-finance-system-for-the-united-states_130841370832.pdf.

[64] P.L. 72-304.

[65] The Financial Institutions Recover, Reform and Enforcement Act of 1989 (FIRREA), P.L. 101-73, made membership optional and allowed a broader range of financial institutions to join.

[66] For more information about the current conforming loan limits, see CRS Report RS22172, *The Conforming Loan Limit*, by N. Eric Weiss and Sean M. Hoskins.

[67] Federal Home Loan Bank Act of 1932, P.L. 72-304, § 17.

[68] Federal National Mortgage Association, U.S. Department of Housing and Urban Development, *Background and History of the Federal National Mortgage Association* (1966).

[69] National Housing Act of 1938, Title III. This is P.L. 75-424.

[70] Treasury could at some later date sell the preferred stock back to Fannie Mae.

[71] National Housing Act of 1954, P.L. 83-50.

[72] Housing and Urban Development Act of 1968, P.L. 90-448, Title VIII, § 801.

[73] U.S. Federal Housing Finance Agency, "FHFA Directs Delisting of Fannie Mae and Freddie Mac Stock from New York Stock Exchange," press release, June 16, 2010, http://www.fhfa.gov/webfiles/15854/Delisting_6_16_10.pdf.

[74] P.L. 101-73.

[75] U.S. Federal Housing Finance Agency, "FHFA Directs Delisting of Fannie Mae and Freddie Mac Stock from New York Stock Exchange," press release, June 16, 2010, http://www.fhfa.gov/webfiles/15854/Delisting_6_16_10.pdf.

In: Mortgages: Policies, Proposals and Trends ISBN: 978-1-62257-689-0
Editors: F. Murphy and O. C. Jensen

Chapter 2

REVISITING MORTGAGE LOAN DISCLOSURES UNDER THE CONSUMER FINANCIAL PROTECTION BUREAU*

Darryl E. Getter and Sean M. Hoskins

SUMMARY

High default and foreclosure rates in the housing market have resulted in questions as to whether borrowers were fully informed about the terms of their mortgage loans. A lack of transparency with respect to loan terms and settlement costs can make it difficult for consumers to make well-informed decisions when choosing mortgage products. In addition, inadequate disclosures can make some borrowers more vulnerable to predatory lending or discriminatory practices.

The adequate disclosure of mortgage terms is a longstanding issue that has prompted several congressional actions. For example, the Truth in Lending Act (TILA) of 1968 and the Real Estate Settlement Procedures Act (RESPA) of 1974 were enacted to require disclosures of credit costs and terms to borrowers. The Economic Growth and Regulatory Paperwork Reduction Act of 1996 (P.L. 104-208) directed the Federal Reserve Board and the Department of Housing and Urban Development (HUD) to propose a single form that satisfied the requirements of RESPA and TILA. However, the Federal Reserve Board

* This is an edited, reformatted and augmented version of Congressional Research Service, Publication No. R41980, dated June 6, 2012.

and HUD concluded that regulatory changes would not be sufficient and that further statutory changes would be required for the forms to be consolidated. More recently, the Dodd-Frank Wall Street Reform and Consumer Protection Act of 2010 (Dodd-Frank Act; P.L. 111-203), which established the Consumer Financial Protection Bureau (CFPB), mandated the new agency revisit disclosure stipulations for mortgage loans. In addition, the Dodd-Frank Act requires the CFPB to consolidate mandatory TILA and RESPA disclosures into one Loan Estimate form.

The 112th Congress has been closely monitoring the subsequent rulemaking associated with the Dodd-Frank Act, as well as the performance and effectiveness of the CFPB. Consequently, this report examines one of the first major actions undertaken by the new agency. Specifically, efforts by the CFPB to create an effective mortgage disclosure form for borrowers are discussed.

INTRODUCTION

Relatively high default and foreclosure rates in the housing market have led some to question whether borrowers were fully informed about the terms of their mortgage loans. There has been concern that mortgage disclosure forms are confusing and not easily understood by borrowers. It has been argued that transparent mortgage terms could enhance consumer shopping and discourage predatory, discriminatory, and fraudulent lending practices. Lending practices that involve hidden costs may result in a payment shock to a borrower, possibly leading to financial distress or even foreclosure.

The issue of adequate disclosure of mortgage terms is longstanding. The Truth in Lending Act (TILA) of 1968, which was previously implemented by the Federal Reserve Board via Regulation Z,[1] requires lenders to disclose the cost of credit and repayment terms of mortgage loans before borrowers enter into any transactions.[2] The TILA Disclosure Statement conveys information about the credit costs and terms of the transaction. The TILA Disclosure Statement lists the annual percentage rate (APR), an interest rate calculation that incorporates both the loan rate and fees. The statement also discloses finance charges, the amount financed, the total number of the payments, whether the interest rate on the mortgage loan can change, and whether the borrower has the option to refinance the loan.

The Real Estate Settlement Procedures Act (RESPA) of 1974 is another element of the consumer disclosure regime. RESPA requires standardized disclosures about the settlement or closing costs, which are costs associated with the acquisition of residential mortgages.[3] Examples of such costs include loan origination fees or points, credit report fees, property appraisal fees, mortgage insurance fees, title insurance fees, home and flood insurance fees, recording fees, attorney fees, and escrow account deposits. In other words, the mortgage loan rate and fees are disclosed in separate calculations rather than in one calculation.

In addition, RESPA, which was implemented by the Department of Housing and Urban Development (HUD),[4] includes the following provisions: (1) providers of settlement services are required to provide a good faith estimate (GFE) of the settlement service costs borrowers should expect at the closing of their mortgage loans;[5] (2) a list of the actual closing costs must be provided to borrowers at the time of closing, which are typically listed on the HUD-1 settlement statement; and (3) RESPA prohibits "referral fees" or "kickbacks" among settlement service providers to prevent settlement fees from increasing unnecessarily.

The Dodd-Frank Wall Street Reform and Consumer Protection Act of 2010 (Dodd-Frank Act; P.L. 111-203) transferred general rulemaking authority for various provisions of TILA and RESPA to a new Consumer Financial Protection Bureau (CFPB)[6] effective July 21, 2011.[7] Lenders currently present borrowers with both TILA and RESPA disclosures, but the Dodd-Frank Act has directed the CFPB to create a single disclosure form that satisfies both disclosure requirements.[8] The CFPB must issue a proposed rule of the new Loan Estimate form within one year of its July 21, 2011 transfer date.[9] The CFPB released two initial Loan Estimate prototypes in May 2011 and has proposed several rounds of updated prototypes since then.[10] This report reviews current efforts to regulate the reporting of pertinent loan information to consumers, including actions taken by the CFPB.[11]

2008 Disclosure Modifications

As previously stated, TILA requires mortgage lenders to present borrowers with a disclosure statement that conveys information about the credit costs and terms of the transaction in one APR calculation expressed as a percentage. TILA was amended in 1980 to require the Federal Reserve to publish APR disclosure forms.[12] On November 17, 2008, HUD made changes to the RESPA component of the mortgage disclosure process that it supervises.[13] Key modifications are discussed below.

Standardizing the Good Faith Estimate Form

HUD's final rule developed a standardized good faith estimate form for use in the initial stages of obtaining mortgages.[14] The GFE included changes intended to help consumers better understand and locate relevant information about their mortgage products. For example, the GFE conveys information about the mortgage terms, whether the interest rate can rise, whether the overall loan balance can rise, whether the loan has a prepayment penalty, whether the loan has a balloon payment, and whether the quoted monthly payment includes a monthly escrow payment for taxes. All of this information about the loan appears on the first page of the GFE.

In addition to facilitating comparison shopping, the HUD GFE form also results in reliable GFEs in the sense that some of the estimated costs are required to not change substantially by the time consumers are ready to close on their loans. Shopping for the best deal or the most affordable loan would be pointless if the costs were to change when borrowers arrived at closing. Consequently, page three of the GFE lists charges that cannot increase, charges that are allowed to increase up to 10%, and charges that may change at settlement. For specific charges that should not change or exceed the 10% limit, a borrower has the option to withdraw the application. This makes it difficult for lenders to generate "costs" or fees that could not be easily justified.

A separate GFE is required for each loan product offered to the borrower. For example, a borrower may wish to compare a traditional fixed rate mortgage (FRM) loan with an adjustable rate mortgage (ARM) loan. Both mortgage products must have separate GFEs to ensure that the information provided is unique to each product. HUD argued that these changes to the GFE would reduce confusion about loan and settlement costs, help the borrower better determine product affordability, and facilitate comparison shopping.[15]

HUD distinguished two stages in the overall mortgage seeking process.[16] The consumer receives a GFE in stage 1, which occurs prior to proceeding with the official mortgage application in stage 2. In the first stage, the lender is not expected to have performed any underwriting, and the GFE need only consist of information obtained from the borrower without any verification of borrower statements. Final underwriting is expected to begin in stage 2 after the borrower has expressed a willingness to proceed with an official mortgage application. The GFE becomes binding only if the underwriting process confirms borrower statements and loan qualifications. If the underwriting process reveals that the borrower is unable to qualify for the specific loan product, then the lender may reject the borrower or propose a new GFE for another loan product in which the borrower is more likely to qualify.

The TILA Disclosure Statement also has a two-stage process similar to the GFE. If the initial APR on the disclosure changes by more than a certain amount after the loan underwriting is performed, the lender must provide a corrected Disclosure Statement at least three days before the loan can be finalized. If a term other than the APR changes after underwriting, then the corrected disclosure must be presented to the borrower at the time the loan is finalized.[17]

For a majority of prime or high-credit quality borrowers, the final loan rates initially stated on the GFE forms are likely to become the actual ones after underwriting. Lenders typically advertise the interest rates that prime borrowers are likely to be charged, and high-credit quality borrowers are arguably already able to shop for loans.[18] Subprime or high-risk borrowers, however, encounter difficulties shopping for loan rates and may continue to do so under this system. Lenders typically charge higher rates to riskier borrowers to compensate for the additional risk, and such rates are typically determined after underwriting has occurred. Hence, low-credit quality borrowers may be less likely to obtain estimates of loan rates prior to final underwriting that would not change afterwards. Assuming no substantial shifts in the current proportion of prime relative to subprime borrowers, or that the share of prime borrowers diminishes as a result of further borrower risk gradations, underwriting at the GFE stage might not be necessary for the vast majority of consumers to obtain fairly reliable pricing information of mortgage products.

A standardized HUD-1 settlement statement is required at all settlements or closings involving mortgage loans. The HUD-1 lists all settlement charges paid at closing, the seller's net proceeds, and the buyer's net payment. HUD modified the HUD-1 form to make it easier for borrowers to trace the estimated costs on the GFE to the actual charges listed on the HUD-1 form. The itemized charges listed on the HUD-1 form include references to the same charges originally listed on the GFE. With these references, it may become more apparent to borrowers what charges remained the same or changed from the estimation stage to the closing stage.

Disclosure of Yield Spread Premium and the Trade-off Table

Prior to implementation of the standardized GFE, a Federal Trade Commission (FTC) study tested 819 consumers to document their understanding of mortgage cost disclosures and loan terms, as well as their ability to avoid deceptive lending practices.[19] The authors found that both prime and subprime borrowers had difficulty understanding important mortgage costs after viewing mortgage cost disclosures. Some borrowers had difficulty identifying the APR of the loan and loan amounts. Many borrowers did not understand why the interest rate and APR of a loan would differ.[20] In addition, borrowers had trouble understanding loan terms for the more complicated mortgage products, such as those with optional credit insurance, interest-only payments, balloon payments, and prepayment penalties. Many borrowers were unable to determine whether balloon payments, prepayment penalties, or up-front loan charges were part of the loan.

The inability to understand a loan offer makes a borrower more vulnerable to predatory lending. Predatory loans are often characterized by high fees or interest rates and other provisions that may not benefit the borrower.[21] Given that one area particularly susceptible to predatory action is the calculation of lender compensation, HUD's revised GFE form includes new disclosure methods so borrowers can understand the fees they are charged to obtain their mortgage loans. Loan charges may be collected either through points (up-front fees), or via the interest rate mechanism, which is referred to as the yield spread premium (YSP), or some combination of these two pricing mechanisms.[22] Page two of the revised standardized GFE form discloses the computation of the total origination costs.[23]

In addition, if borrowers realize that mortgage loan origination costs may be collected by some combination of up-front fees and YSP, then they may also realize that it is possible to choose between paying higher up-front fees for a lower interest rate or lower up-front fees for a higher interest rate. Recognition of this trade-off may help borrowers avoid being charged both higher rates and higher fees. The GFE includes a trade-off table on page three to facilitate the understanding of the trade-off between interest rates and points. The trade-off table discloses how a loan with the same principal face value and a lower interest rate results in higher up-front settlement costs; it also discloses how the same loan with a higher interest rate results in lower up-front settlement costs.

Although the trade-off table was found to benefit consumers,[24] HUD's final rule required only the leftmost column of the table to be filled out. The decision to allow loan originators the option to fill out the remaining columns was related to concerns regarding the cost burden and time to calculate comparable loan costs information.[25] In addition, the trade-off table may still be difficult to interpret for loans with adjustable interest rates, which are likely to change over the life of the loan and distort the inverse relationship between the interest rate and up-front fees. Some borrowers, however, may be inclined to request that loan originators fill out the table completely, which would facilitate HUD's policy objectives to achieve transparency.[26]

RECENT CFPB PROPOSALS

As required by the Dodd-Frank Act, the CFPB has proposed various prototypes of a standardized Loan Estimate form to combine the TILA Disclosure Statement and HUD's GFE into a single document.[27] The Dodd-Frank Act directed the CFPB to issue a proposed rule of the new Loan Estimate form within one year of its July 21, 2011 transfer date.[28] The CFPB stated its plans to perform five rounds of testing in six different cities before the final rule is proposed.[29] In addition to consumer testing, the CFPB also stated that it will convene a Small Business Review Panel to solicit feedback on its prototype.[30] The current prototype, Tupelo, is the most recent form available on the CFPB website and has been developed after at least five rounds of testing.[31]

Tupelo has three pages with the first page containing three sections.[32] The first section presents the loan amount; the interest rate and whether it can change; the monthly loan payment; and whether a prepayment penalty or a balloon payment exists. The second section discloses the projected monthly payments over various time periods of the loan. Estimates of the borrower's monthly payment also includes estimated property taxes, insurance, and assessments. This section also shows whether an escrow account exists and how much the borrower should expect to pay each month. The last section on page one provides the estimated amount needed to close.

The second page of the Tupelo prototype uses the example of a loan for $211,000 with $6,151 in closing costs for the sake of illustrating a completed form. The prototype has five sections. The first two sections itemize the various expenses associated with closing.[33] The third section calculates the cash needed to close by summing the settlement fees, settlement costs, down payment, and other costs. Next, a table provides the potential borrower with information on the monthly payments, such as whether there are any interest-only payments and what the maximum payment could be. Finally, a second table describes whether the mortgage interest rate is adjustable and how it could potentially change.

The third page of the Tupelo prototype contains three additional sections. The first section allows borrowers to compare the terms of other loans offered by other loan originators.[34] The section lists the amount that a borrower will have paid in total over the first five years of the loan and how much would go to paying down principal. It also lists the APR as well as the total amount of interest paid over the loan term as a percentage of the loan. The next section provides brief information about other aspects (e.g., appraisal, homeowner's insurance, late payments, and servicing). Should the borrower decide to proceed with the mortgage origination process, the final section provides a space for the applicant to sign to confirm that the form was received.

The CFPB has also developed a prototype settlement disclosure,[35] which consolidates the HUD-1 Settlement Statement and the final TILA disclosure.[36]

End Notes

[1] The primary rulemaking and enforcement authority of many existing consumer protection laws was transferred to the CFPB by the Dodd-Frank Act. See CRS Report R41338, *The Dodd-Frank Wall Street Reform and Consumer Protection Act: Title X, The Consumer Financial Protection Bureau*, by David H. Carpenter.

[2] TILA is contained in Title I of the Consumer Credit Protection Act, P.L. 90-301, 81 Stat. 146, as amended by 15 U.S.C. Section 1601 et seq.

[3] P.L. 93-533, 88 Stat. 1724, 12 U.S.C. Sections 2601-2617.

[4] The primary rulemaking and enforcement authority of many existing consumer protection laws was transferred to the CFPB by the Dodd-Frank Act. See CRS Report R41338, *The Dodd-Frank Wall Street Reform and Consumer Protection Act: Title X, The Consumer Financial Protection Bureau*, by David H. Carpenter.

[5] The GFE never discusses loan details using the APR term, which is only required on the TILA Disclosure Statement.

[6] For more on the CFPB, see CRS Report R41338, *The Dodd-Frank Wall Street Reform and Consumer Protection Act: Title X, The Consumer Financial Protection Bureau*, by David H. Carpenter.

[7] Bureau of Consumer Financial Protection, "Identification of Enforceable Rules and Orders," 76 *Federal Register* 43569, July 21, 2011.

[8] P.L. 111-203, Section 1098, 12 U.S.C Section 2603.

[9] However, Dodd-Frank states that the bureau does not have to produce a proposed rule if "the Bureau determines that any proposal issued by the Board of Governors and the Secretary of Housing and Urban Development carries out the same purpose." See P.L. 111-203, Section 1032(f).

[10] See Bureau of Consumer Financial Protection, "Know Before You Owe," at http://www .consumerfinance.gov/ knowbeforeyouowe/.

[11] One purpose of simplified disclosure forms is to facilitate consumers' comparison shopping for loan terms. For more information on the extent to which consumers shop to obtain the best

mortgage terms, see CRS Report RL 34442, *HUD Proposes Administrative Modifications to the Real Estate Settlement Procedures Act*, by Darryl E. Getter.

[12] P.L. 96-221, 94 Stat. 170, 15 U.S.C. 1604.

[13] Department of Housing and Urban Development, "Real Estate Settlement Procedures Act (RESPA): Rule To Simplify and Improve the Process of Obtaining Mortgages and Reduce Consumer Settlement Costs," 73 *Federal Register* 68204, November 17, 2008.

[14] Department of Housing and Urban Development, "Good Faith Estimate (GFE)," at http://portal.hud.gov/hudportal/ documents/huddoc?id=gfestimate.pdf.

[15] HUD tested the GFE form among various consumer groups; details about these tests may be found at http://www.hud.gov/offices/hsg/sfh/res/200803/summary.pdf.

[16] Department of Housing and Urban Development, "Real Estate Settlement Procedures Act (RESPA): Proposed Rule To Simplify and Improve the Process of Obtaining Mortgages and Reduce Consumer Settlement Costs," 73 *Federal Register* 14035, March 14, 2008.

[17] Federal Reserve System, "Truth In Lending," 74 *Federal Register* 43232, August 26, 2009.

[18] See Patricia A. McCoy, "Rethinking Disclosure in a World of Risk-Based Pricing," *Harvard Journal on Legislation*, vol. 44, no. 1, winter 2007.

[19] James M. Lacko and Janis K. Pappalardo, *Improving Consumer Mortgage Disclosures: An Empirical Assessment of Current and Prototype Disclosure Forms*, Bureau of Economics Staff Report, Federal Trade Commission, June 2007, at http://www.ftc.gov/ os/2007/06/P025505MortgageDisclosureReport.pdf.

[20] The APR is the annual cost of a loan, which includes the interest cost of the principal loan amount, insurance, and other fees expressed as a percentage. The mortgage interest rate only includes the interest cost of the principal loan amount expressed as a percentage.

[21] High interest rates and fees may be characteristic of predatory lending but not all loans with high interest rates and fees are predatory. Some borrowers with poor credit histories may have to accept high rates if they wish to borrow from any lender. For more on the complications of defining predatory lending, see James H. Carr and Lopa Kolluri, *Predatory Lending: An Overview*, Fannie Mae Foundation, 2001.

[22] The mortgage interest rate and the YSP are not identical. The YSP is defined as the difference between the total coupon interest rate and the actual wholesale interest rate of the loan. For example, a loan with a market or wholesale rate of 6% may have a total coupon rate of 6.5%, and 0.5% is the compensation going to the mortgage broker, which is the YSP. Some mortgage lenders may pay brokers up to 2% in YSP.

[23] On page two of the revised standardized GFE form, the total origination costs are disclosed in item 1. The division of these costs into points and YSP is disclosed in item 2. A "credit" that represents the dollar value of loan origination costs *not paid at settlement* appears in item 2. In this context, "credit" does not mean the borrower would receive a refund from the loan originator. Instead, credit refers to the loan origination costs that the borrower still pays, not up front at settlement, but in the form of a higher interest rate, or the YSP. Conversely, the dollar value of fees paid up front at settlement appears as a "charge" in item 2. For a given interest rate, both credit and charge amounts in item 2 should add up to the total loan origination costs, which appears in item 1. The adjusted origination costs, which appear in box A, are the difference between the total loan origination costs and the YSP; the adjusted origination costs refers to the amount of total upfront fees that will be paid at settlement.

[24] HUD's testing concluded that 90% of the consumers understood how the trade-off table worked and stated that it was the most useful aspect of the GFE. See Department of Housing and Urban Development, *RESPA: Regulatory Impact Analysis and Initial*

Regulatory Flexibility Analysis, FR-5180 5180-F-02, p. 176, at http://www.hud.gov/offices/hsg/ ramh/res/impactanalysis.pdf.

[25] HUD estimates that if the GFE added 10 minutes per application, then annual national costs would increase by $255 million if there are 1.7 applications per loan or by $405 million if there are 2.7 applications per loan. Calculations used a $150,000 annual salary and a 2,080 hour work year to determine the hourly wage, which was then scaled to the actual time needed to fill out the forms. See Department of Housing and Urban Development, *RESPA: Regulatory Impact Analysis and Initial Regulatory Flexibility Analysis*, FR-5180 5180-F-02, at http://www.hud.gov/offices/hsg/ramh/res/ impactanalysis.pdf.

[26] Participants in the HUD study expressed suspicion when the trade-off table was not filled in completely. See http://www.hud.gov/offices/hsg/ramh/res/impactanalysis.pdf, p. 190. In 2009, the state of New Hampshire mandated that the entire trade-off table be completed whenever a yield spread premium is to be collected. If a corresponding loan (with lower settlement charges and a higher interest rate or a lower interest rate and higher settlement charges) is unavailable, the lender fills in "N/A." See New Hampshire Banking Department, "Newsletter," at http://www.nh.gov/banking/News letterIssue09_2.pdf.

[27] P.L. 104-208, the Economic Growth and Regulatory Paperwork Reduction Act of 1996, directed HUD and the Federal Reserve Board to propose a single form that satisfied the requirements of RESPA and TILA. The Federal Reserve Board and HUD concluded that regulatory changes would not be sufficient and that further statutory changes would be required for the forms to be consolidated. The Dodd-Frank Act provided the necessary legislative authority. See Federal Reserve System, "Truth in Lending," 63 *Federal Register* 6112, February 6, 1998.

[28] However, Dodd-Frank states that the bureau does not have to produce a proposed rule if "the Bureau determines that any proposal issued by the Board of Governors and the Secretary of Housing and Urban Development carries out the same purpose." See P.L. 111-203, Section 1032(f).

[29] See Consumer Financial Protection Bureau, "Know Before You Owe," at http://www.consumerfinance.gov/knowbefore-you-owe-designing-a-new-disclosure/.

[30] See Consumer Financial Protection Bureau, "SBREFA, Small Providers, and Mortgage Disclosure," at http://www.consumerfinance.gov/blog/sbrefa-small-providers-and-mortgage-disclosure/.

[31] On May 18, 2011, the first two prototypes were made available on the CFPB's website. The Ficus form may be found at http://www.consumerfinance.gov/wp-content/uploads/2011/05/disclosure1.pdf; the Pecan form may be found at http://www.consumerfinance.gov/wp-content/uploads/2011/05/disclosure2.pdf. Other prototypes are also available on the CFPB website. The CFPB website does not provide detailed information on the substance of the comments they have received about the prototypes, nor does it provide an explanation as to why different versions of the prototypes have been altered.

[32] The three page Tupelo document combines the two page TILA Disclosure Statement and three page HUD GFE.

[33] HUD's original GFE lists whether fees can change, can change only by a certain amount, or cannot change between the time they are listed on the GFE and closing. The Tupelo prototype lists what services a borrower can or cannot shop for but does not list tolerances to show how much some fees can increase before closing as is done on the current GFE.

[34] Unlike the GFE, the Tupelo prototype does not include a trade-off table.

[35] See Consumer Financial Protection Bureau, "Know Before You Owe: The last dance... or is it?" at http://www.consumerfinance.gov/blog/know-before-you-owe-the-last-dance-or-is-it/.

[36] The HUD-1 Settlement Statement is the form borrowers receive at the closing that lists all final settlement charges. The HUD-1 Settlement Statement was revised by HUD to be compatible with the numbers provided on its GFE form so that making the comparisons would be easier for borrowers.

In: Mortgages: Policies, Proposals and Trends ISBN: 978-1-62257-689-0
Editors: F. Murphy and O. C. Jensen

Chapter 3

ABILITY TO REPAY, RISK-RETENTION STANDARDS, AND MORTGAGE CREDIT ACCESS*

Darryl E. Getter

SUMMARY

Prior to the recent financial crisis, mortgage underwriting standards were relaxed to the point where many borrowers could only repay their loans if favorable financial conditions that existed at the time of origination remained intact. In other words, borrowers obtained mortgage loans that relied upon interest rates not rising or the value of the underlying collateral (house prices) not declining. When market conditions changed, however, many mortgage loans became delinquent and went into default. The mortgage defaults often translated into large losses for both the borrowers and the financial industry.

After enactment of The Dodd-Frank Wall Street Reform and Consumer Protection Act of 2010 (Dodd-Frank Act; P.L. 111-203), the Federal Reserve Board announced a proposed qualified mortgage (QM) rule that would establish "ability to repay" standards for mortgage lending. The Federal Reserve, along with other federal regulatory agencies, also jointly released a proposed risk retention or qualified residential mortgage (QRM) rule to require

* This is an edited, reformatted and augmented version of the Congressional Research Service Publication, CRS Report for Congress R42056, dated June 5, 2012.

parties involved in a transaction in which mortgage originations are sold to retain "skin-in-the-game" or a minimum percentage of the credit risk of financial products, which would result in the sharing of any eventual losses. Adoption of ability to repay and risk-retention standards may discourage lenders from excessively relaxing lending standards even during economic boom periods, thus making loan repayment more resilient to sudden shifts in short-term economic and financial conditions.

The ability to repay and risk-retention standards, while designed to curtail the pre-crisis proliferation of risky lending practices, are likely to simultaneously reduce access to mortgage credit. Although ability-to-repay standards would encourage consistent underwriting at all times, some borrowers that benefit from lender flexibility during more favorable macroeconomic conditions are likely to face increased difficulty obtaining mortgage loans. Lenders may be reluctant to originate loans that are not in compliance with the ability-to-repay standards if this exposes them to increased legal risks. Likewise, risk-retention standards that translate into more stringent qualification requirements for borrowers are likely to increase barriers to homeownership for both creditworthy and disadvantaged borrowers.

The 112th Congress is overseeing the rulemaking stemming from the Dodd-Frank Act. This report examines the developments associated with the implementation of mortgage lending reforms. After summarizing the proposed ability to repay and risk-retention standards, a description of risky underwriting practices that occurred prior to the mortgage crisis is presented, followed by a discussion of possible effects on mortgage credit accessibility.

The Consumer Financial Protection Bureau (CFPB), which will prescribe final regulations on QM rule, has re-opened the comment period to seek further comments on the litigation risks that could potentially arise from the new requirements. The comments, however, should be narrowly focused and based upon analysis that uses mortgage data provided by the regulator of Fannie Mae and Freddie Mac. The closing date for comments will be July 9, 2012.

INTRODUCTION

Prior to the recent financial crisis, mortgage underwriting standards were relaxed to the point where many borrowers could only repay their loans if the favorable financial conditions that existed at the time of origination remained intact. In other words, borrowers were able to obtain mortgage loans that relied upon interest rates not rising or the value of the underlying collateral (house prices) not declining. When market conditions changed, however, many mortgage loans became delinquent and went into default. The mortgage defaults often translated into large losses for both the borrowers and the financial industry.

"Irrational exuberance," a term coined by then-Federal Reserve Chairman Alan Greenspan, arguably captures the essence of the academic work of Hyman Minsky[1] and has been used to illustrate the dynamics that contributed to the recent financial crisis. According to Minsky, when lenders grow excessively optimistic, they increase credit availability as if the ideal economic and financial market conditions will persist. Lender optimism during the height of a business cycle can translate into a substantial increase in debt accumulation or "leveraging" by the private sector. Moreover, leveraging in response to a particular asset market bubble can result in overinvestment into a particular sector (such as housing) as well as numerous financial portfolios lacking diversification outside of one broad asset class. A "Minsky moment" subsequently occurs when assets are unable to continue generating the level of revenues necessary to repay the loans that were used to purchase them. In other words, the expected future value of the collateral used to secure the loan fails to increase and may even decline, and the borrower lacks the income stream or the ability to sell the asset to repay the outstanding loan balance. Recessions that occur after individuals have accumulated large levels of debt, therefore, are likely to be more severe than those characterized by lower debt levels. An escalation of defaults is likely to occur after a proliferation of leveraged investments have gone sour, which debilitates the banking system and impedes any subsequent lending necessary to stimulate recovery.

Rulemaking is now taking place to implement "ability to repay" and risk-retention standards as mandated by the Dodd-Frank Wall Street Reform and Consumer Protection Act of 2010 (Dodd-Frank Act; P.L. 111-203). Under the Dodd-Frank Act, mortgage originators are required to make a good faith determination that a borrower has a reasonable ability to repay the loan regardless of the prevailing financial conditions. In addition, parties involved in a securitization[2] transaction must retain "skin-in-the-game" or a minimum percentage of the credit risk, which would further encourage greater due diligence given the sharing of any eventual losses. Hence, the ability to repay and risk-retention measures address some risky financial practices that arguably contributed to recent excessive mortgage debt accumulation and subsequent financial crisis.

The ability to repay and risk-retention standards would dampen any future periods of rapid mortgage debt accumulation by encouraging lenders to adopt qualification standards higher than those that existed prior to the financial crisis. Although some borrowers may qualify for loans when underwriting criteria are relaxed, which typically may occur at times when housing and macroeconomic conditions are more favorable for repayment, lenders may be reluctant to originate those that fail to comply with qualification standards that would reduce their exposures to legal risks. Hence, some creditworthy borrowers may be unable to obtain mortgage credit.

The 112th Congress is monitoring the rulemaking stemming from the Dodd-Frank Act. This report examines the developments associated with the implementation of mortgage lending reforms. The report begins with a summary of proposed ability to repay and risk-retention standards. Next, the report describes risky underwriting and financing practices that occurred prior to the mortgage crisis, followed by a discussion of how access to mortgage credit might be affected.

OVERVIEW OF REGULATORY ACTIONS

This section provides an overview of the proposed rules having to do with the ability to repay and risk-retention standards. Regulatory reforms will require creditors to consider whether borrowers have the ability to repay loans, and loan originators will also have to adhere to stricter underwriting or borrower qualification standards if they choose to sell loans to securitizers. Ability to repay and risk-retention standards are designed to provide lenders and securitizers with legal protection when they refrain from lending practices that weaken overall financial stability as well as to protect borrowers from assuming mortgage obligations that are affordable only under certain circumstances.

Ability to Repay Standards and Qualified Mortgages

Title XIV of the Dodd-Frank Act is entitled the Mortgage Reform and Anti-Predatory Lending Act; Section 1411 is entitled "Ability to Repay" and says,

> In accordance with regulations prescribed by the (Federal Reserve) Board, no creditor may make a residential mortgage loan unless the creditor makes a reasonable and good faith determination based on verified and documented information that, at the time the loan is consummated, the consumer has a reasonable ability to repay the loan, according to its terms, and all applicable taxes, insurance (including mortgage guarantee insurance), and assessments.

Minimum standards for residential mortgage loan originations, which consist of factors that creditors are required to consider during the underwriting process, are established beginning in Section 1411 and subsequent sections of the Dodd-Frank Act.

On April 19, 2011, the Federal Reserve, as mandated by the Dodd-Frank Act, announced a proposed rule that would require all creditors or lenders to make a good faith estimate that a borrower has a reasonable ability to repay. The rule would also establish minimum mortgage underwriting standards.[3] The rule would expand ability-to-repay standards to cover all residential mortgage loans. The Dodd-Frank Act transferred the authority to prescribe final regulations to the Consumer Financial Protection Bureau (CFPB) on July 21, 2011, and the closing date for comments was July 22, 2011. The CFPB has re-opened the comment period to seek further comments on the litigation risks that could potentially arise from the new requirements.[4] The comments, however, should be narrowly focused and based upon analysis that uses mortgage data from the portfolios of Fannie Mae and Freddie Mac, which are discussed in more detail below. The closing date for comments will be July 9, 2012. CFPB final rulemaking would not necessarily be bound by the Federal Reserve's proposed regulation.[5]

The proposed rule provides four methods in which a lender would be able to comply with the ability-to-repay standards. First, the originator can meet a general ability-to-repay standard by considering and verifying the following criteria: income or assets, current employment status, the size of the monthly mortgage payment, any monthly payment of subordinate or junior mortgages, the monthly payments of related mortgage expenses, other debt obligations, the monthly debt-to-income ratios, and credit history. In addition, creditors would be required to calculate the mortgage payment using the fully indexed rate. In other words, even if the borrower selects a nontraditional mortgage product with an initial lower interest rate, the adjustable interest rate plus the margin (the "mark-up" over the short-term interest rate index or constant amount added to the variable interest rate) must be used during underwriting.

This compliance option does not place restrictions on the loan features, terms, or points and fees.

Second, a lender can be in compliance by refinancing borrowers out of nonstandard and into standard mortgage products. Standard mortgage products are defined as those without negative amortization features, interest-only payments, or balloon payments. They also have limits on points and fees. This compliance option allows for streamlined refinances that can quickly move borrowers out of higher risk mortgages and into ones with more stable payments. In addition, lenders would not have to verify the income and assets for borrowers being switched into standard mortgage products as long as their new monthly payments will be lower and they have not experienced delinquencies while paying their existing mortgages.

The third compliance option reduces regulatory burdens and legal liability exposure for originators and assignees holding "qualified mortgage" (QM) loans. The Federal Reserve proposed two alternative definitions for QMs given the inability to determine whether Congress intended the legal protection to be in the form of a *safe harbor or a rebuttable presumption*. The first definition, Alternative 1, operates as a *safe harbor*, which means that borrowers would not be able to assert that creditors failed to comply with any of the required underwriting criteria described below. The second definition, Alternative 2, operates as a *rebuttable presumption* of compliance, which allows borrowers to provide evidence that may possibly overturn a presumption of lender compliance even if the required procedures were followed.[6]

The definition of a QM loan under Alternative 1 excludes mortgages with negative amortization features, interest-only payments, balloon payments, or terms that exceed 30 years. In addition, the total points and fees cannot exceed 3% of the total loan amount (for loans of $75,000 or more). The income and assets of the borrower must be verified. The underwriting of the mortgage must be based upon the maximum interest rate that might occur during the first five years, use a fully amortizing payment schedule, and incorporate other mortgage-related obligations such as escrows for property taxes. Under Alternative 2, lenders must still comply with all criteria listed under the first definition. In addition, employment status, credit history, debt-to-income ratio, and other debt repayment obligations must be considered during underwriting.

The final compliance option allows a lender to originate a balloon-payment QM in predominantly rural or underserved areas. A mortgage with a balloon payment is one in which regular payments are made for a period of time; but given that the payments include only partial or no amortization of the principal balance, the final payment that includes the remaining balance may be considerably larger. A balloon loan can be a QM as long as it is not a higher-priced loan, has a minimum term of five years, and the borrower must be qualified on the maximum possible payment that could occur over the first five years of the loan.[7]

Risk-Retention Standards and Qualified Residential Mortgages

Title IX Subtitle D of the Dodd-Frank Act is entitled "Improvements to the Asset-Backed Securitization Process"; Section 941 is entitled "Regulation of Credit Risk Retention." This section requires securitizers to retain "not less than 5 percent of the credit risk for any asset that is not a qualified residential mortgage…" The Dodd-Frank Act authorizes the Federal Reserve and other financial regulatory agencies to implement requirements to ensure that relevant parties involved in a securitization transaction retain "skin-in-the-game" or a requirement to ensure the sharing of potential losses.[8] The legislation requires the agencies to jointly define the term *qualified residential mortgage*. The agencies must also take into consideration "underwriting and product features that historical loan performance data indicate result in a lower risk of default," including some factors cited in the legislation.

On April 29, 2011, six financial regulatory agencies published a proposed rule that would apply to securitized loans; the closing date for comments was August 1, 2011.[9] Securitizers would be required to retain at least 5% of the credit or default risk of the underlying mortgage assets that constitute the security.[10] The risk-retention requirement, however, would not apply to loans insured by the Federal Housing Administration (FHA) or the government-sponsored enterprises (GSEs) Fannie Mae or Freddie Mac while they are under conservatorship.[11] The securitizer may also be exempted from the risk-retention requirement if the underlying assets meet the qualified residential mortgage (QRM) standards, which are stricter than the requirements for QM loans under the proposed rule.[12]

Mortgages exempted from the risk-retention requirements feature higher qualification requirements on borrowers. QRMs must be closed-end first-lien mortgages to purchase or refinance a one-to-four unit family property in which at least one unit is the principal residence of the borrower. In addition, homebuyers must also put down at least 20% of the purchase price in addition to paying the closing costs, 25% for standard mortgage refinancings, and 30% for cash-out refinancings that allow borrowers to extract equity from their homes.[13] Mortgages having such characteristics are exempt from risk-retention requirements given that the probability of default is significantly lower relative to mortgages in which borrowers have lower downpayments.

In addition, the definition of a QRM loan also excludes negative amortization features, interest-only payments, balloon payments, junior liens, prepayment penalties, or terms exceeding 30 years. The total points and fees cannot exceed 3% of the total loan amount. The income and assets of the borrower must be considered and verified. The underwriting of the mortgage must be based upon the maximum interest rate that might occur during the first five years, use a fully amortizing payment schedule, and incorporate other mortgage-related obligations, such as escrows for property taxes. For adjustable rate mortgages, the interest rates cannot increase more than 2% per year or 6% over the life of the loans. The employment status, credit history, debt-to-income ratio, and other debt repayment obligations of the borrowers must also be considered and verified. The borrowers' front- and back-end ratios must be at least 28% and 36%, respectively.[14] Borrowers cannot currently be 30 days past due on any loan obligation; have been 60 days delinquent on any loan obligation within the past two years; or be in bankruptcy, a short sale, foreclosure, or other federal or state judgment for the collection of any unpaid debts within the last three years. QRMs must be supported by written appraisals, and loan servicers must perform loss mitigation (or offer borrower workout options) in the event of default.

Table 1 provides an abbreviated summary of differences between the QM and QRM requirements. As stated earlier, the QRM requirements for securitized mortgages that would be exempted from the risk-retention rule are stricter than the QM requirements.

Risky Mortgage Underwriting and Financing Practices (Type 1 Errors)

The typical errors that occur in mortgage lending can be characterized using a standard statistical framework.[15] Suppose a "type 1 error" occurs when borrowers who are likely to have repayment problems receive loans; a "type 2 error" occurs when borrowers who are likely to repay their loans on time are denied credit. In this context, extending credit to unqualified borrowers (type 1 errors) can translate into substantial costs to lenders and foster a rise in aggregate indebtedness that makes both borrowers and lenders vulnerable to a sudden weakening of economic conditions. On the other hand, not extending credit to qualified borrowers (type 2 errors) may translate into forgone profit opportunities for lenders, although there would be no realized losses. The consequences of making type 1 errors are considered worse for lenders (and taxpayers, should numerous mortgage defaults result in federal interventions designed to stabilize financial markets) than type 2 errors. The consequences of type 2 errors, however, include less credit availability for qualified borrowers, which may impede overall economic recovery. In short, the framework illustrates a trade-off that exists between curtailing risky lending practices and borrower access to mortgage credit.

Table 1. Abbreviated Comparison of QM and QRM Requirements

Requirements	Qualified Mortgage (QM)	Qualified Residential Mortgage (QRM)
Banned Mortgage Product Features	Negative amortization loans, interest only, balloon payments	Negative amortization loans, interest only, balloon payments, junior liens, prepayment penalties
Points and Fees	May not exceed 3% of the total loan amount for loans of $75,000 or more	May not exceed 3% of the total loan amount
Underwriting at Fully Indexed Interest Rates	Loan must be underwritten using the maximum interest rate that would occur in the first 5 years after the loan becomes legally binding (usually at closing)	Loan must be underwritten using the maximum interest rate that would occur in the first 5 years after the first loan payment is due
Income or Assets	Consider and verify	Consider and verify
Employment Status	No specific requirement	Consider and verify
Front-end/Back-end Ratios	No specific requirement	28%, 36%
Credit History	No specific requirement	Current on all debts; no 60 day delinquencies in past 2 years; no bankruptcies or foreclosures in past 3 years
Downpayment Requirements	No specific requirements	20% home purchase; 25% standard refinance, 30% cash-out refinance

Source: Philadelphia Federal Reserve Bank at http://www.philadelphiafed.org/bank-resources/publications/consumer-compliance-outlook/outlook-live/2011/052611.pdf

Various high-risk underwriting practices, such as collateral-dependent lending, low- or no-documentation loans, and failure to escrow for property taxes, were common prior to July 14, 2008.[16] Borrowers were also qualified for adjustable rate mortgages (ARMs) based upon the initial interest rate, which does not take into consideration that the loan rate applicable at the time of origination could increase. In addition, many mortgages were held in the portfolios of institutions that held little capital to buffer against a sudden multitude of defaults. Many participants involved in various stages of the securitized lending chain may have failed to perform the level of due diligence that could have revealed relaxed or inadequate underwriting standards. The lending practices discussed in this section arguably are associated with an increase in type 1 errors prior to the financial crisis. These practices or some variation thereof, which existed in prime and nonprime (and subprime) lending markets, allowed the balance sheets of many households and financial institutions to become highly leveraged with mortgage debt that could not be repaid under the economic and financial conditions that prevailed after loan origination.[17]

Collateral-Dependent Lending

The term *collateral-dependent* lending was used to describe loans in which repayment depended more upon the current or expected future value of the housing assets rather than the borrowers' ability to repay using their incomes and savings. In other words, if borrowers lacked the income and other financial resources to meet repayment obligations, the sale of their homes would generate the funds to repay their mortgages. For example, suppose a borrower obtained a mortgage with an initial interest-only feature over a short period that might satisfy front- and back-end ratios at the time of origination. Once the interest-only period expired and principal amortization increased the monthly payments, the borrower may no longer satisfy the minimum front-end requirements. As long as house prices rose or did not substantially decline, the borrower could either refinance into another interest-only mortgage or sell the home at a price sufficient to satisfy the outstanding debt obligation. This practice allowed borrowers to take on large amounts of debt that could only be repaid under favorable economic conditions.

Collateral-dependent lending may also take the form of extremely low or zero downpayment lending. During the 2000s, piggyback or junior or secondary mortgage loans became a popular financing alternative to purchasing mortgage insurance.[18] Piggyback loans offered borrowers at least two advantages. First, the interest on both the primary and secondary mortgages was tax deductible; until 2007, mortgage insurance premiums were not tax deductible.[19] Second, a borrower could transform a jumbo loan into two loans.[20] A conventional conforming loan, which normally would carry a lower interest rate than a jumbo loan, would serve as the primary loan and be combined with a secondary piggyback loan. Although secondary loans are likely to carry rates higher than jumbo rates, the smaller outstanding balance may cause the combined payments of the primary and secondary loans to be smaller than a jumbo payment with private mortgage insurance. The combined payment may be smaller still after factoring in both mortgage interest deductions, which would make the piggyback financing arrangement even more attractive to borrowers.[21]

The piggyback financing arrangement was also popular for borrowers that were not using mortgage credit to purchase homes.[22] "Cash-out refinances" allowed borrowers to pull most or all of the equity out of their homes to make home improvements, which might allow them to increase the marketability and profitability of their homes in the future. Borrowers with various student loan, automobile, credit card, or perhaps medical debts could also take advantage of rapidly rising house prices to consolidate these debts and ultimately reduce monthly payments, lower the interest costs, and improve their credit scores. Hence, while collateral-dependent lending in the form of cash-out refinances allowed some borrowers to speculate on house prices, it also served as a debt-consolidation mechanism that improved cash flow for some highly leveraged borrowers prior to the market decline.

Lien holders, however, grew more exposed to default risk as highly leveraged borrowers had less and less capacity to repay their debt obligations in the event of house price declines. An unexpected decline in house prices could cause borrower debt obligations to suddenly become greater in value than the underlying collateral secured by the loans, and the proceeds from a short or foreclosure sale would not be sufficient to repay loans in full. Underwriting mortgages based upon an assumption that favorable housing market conditions are indefinitely sustainable, therefore, would be considered a risky lending practice. Hence, lenders that relaxed their underwriting standards and relied on rising house prices for loan repayment arguably were speculating in the housing market alongside some borrowers.

The proposed QM rules may discourage lenders from excessively relaxing lending standards even during economic boom periods, thus making loan repayment more resilient to sudden shifts in short-term economic and financial conditions. Under the proposed definition of QRMs, lenders would be exempt from risk retention of any credit risk if the borrower has enough equity to avoid a piggyback financing arrangement. Hence, if the mortgage industry were to adopt a 20% downpayment requirement, then distressed borrowers might still be able to repay the outstanding mortgage balances by selling their homes particularly as long as house prices do not fall by more than 20%.

Low- or No-Documentation Lending

Borrowers generally must provide proof of employment and income when applying for mortgage loans. A letter from an employer or copies of pay slips are typically acceptable ways of verification. Borrowers who are self-employed or paid on commission, however, may lack traditional verification documentation such as employer payment stubs. Hence, low- or no-documentation lending, which did not require traditional documentation but may have required some borrowers to meet higher downpayment requirements, may have benefitted borrowers with nonstandard employment circumstances.

"Low-doc" and "no-doc" loans have nevertheless become referred to as "liar loans" because the financial capacity of a borrower to repay a mortgage can be misrepresented either by the borrower, the lender, or both parties. Dishonest borrowers can mislead lenders, and lenders can intentionally or inadvertently mislead investors. Requiring full-income documentation reduces the likelihood that borrower repayment capacity will be exaggerated or misrepresented. Hence, low-or no-documentation lending is considered a risky underwriting practice.[23]

The increase in use of low- and no-documentation loans during the housing boom may be attributed to several factors. As credit scores evolved as a reliable predictor of default, lenders may have assigned new weights to the various borrower characteristics used when predicting default probabilities. For example, weights assigned to credit history may have increased simultaneously while the weights assigned to income declined.[24] Advances in automated underwriting technology may have influenced the underwriting process to allow for some higher-risk factors if sufficiently compensated by factors that were thought to reduce default risk.[25] In particular, rising house prices or collateral values may have acted as a compensating factor or hedge against borrower defaults. The rise in low- or no-documentation lending, therefore, may arguably be another manifestation of collateral-dependent lending. Given that low- or no- documentation loans would not satisfy the income and asset verification requirements proposed QM and QRM rules, this lending practice would be discouraged.

Qualifying Borrowers on Low, Unadjusted Interest Rates

During 2004-2006, nontraditional loans, as compared with the traditional or standard 30-year fixed rate mortgages, were common. Many of these loans were ARMs with initially low or "teaser" rates; some also had interest-only periods, during which the borrower's payment did not reduce the principal balance of the loan. Even if interest rates do not rise, interest-only loans eventually will have higher payments once the principal repayment period starts. Mortgages with two- or three-year introductory periods, known as 2/28s and 3/27s, proliferated between 2005 and 2006, in particular in the subprime market. "Option ARMs," also called negative amortization loans, would allow borrowers to pay less than the current interest due and also result in higher outstanding debt balances for borrowers choosing to pay only the monthly minimum in the introductory period.

Borrowers can benefit from nontraditional mortgage products if they do not intend to stay in the mortgage for a full 30 years and want to reduce their monthly payments. The required monthly payments on these products are usually lower for an introductory period of time, and the borrower may plan to refinance the mortgage or sell the home before the deferred interest or principal (that would have been paid under a traditional mortgage) becomes due. Hence, nontraditional mortgage products may increase affordability and *reduce* potential repayment problems in some circumstances for borrowers, in particular those who diligently build liquid reserves by saving the difference between the traditional fixed rate and nontraditional mortgage payments (assuming the nontraditional payment is lower).

Nontraditional mortgages, however, are more susceptible to repayment problems associated with sudden changes in financial and economic circumstances. For example, mortgage loans payments that were tied to short-term LIBOR increased after a sudden spike in LIBOR rates in 2008.[26] In addition, repayment problems would be exacerbated for borrowers who lacked sufficient precautionary liquid assets. Borrowers who marginally qualify for nontraditional loans at initially low rates (that may not even include the lender "mark-up" or margin) that would prevail for only a short period of time may be especially vulnerable to future repayment problems. Hence, extending credit with the presumption that the initial interest rates will not rise significantly over the period borrowers are expected to stay in the loan contracts would be considered a risky lending practice. The proposed QM rule requires using the fully indexed interest rate during underwriting, and thus discourages the practice of qualifying borrowers at initially low rates.

Failure to Escrow for Property Taxes

When property taxes are included as part of the mortgage underwriting process, it reduces the likelihood that borrowers are unprepared to pay when tax bills come due. Some first-time home buyers, in particular, may not understand that property taxes are assessed annually, so a tax bill might find them unprepared. Repayment problems are often triggered by some unanticipated expense.[27] Similarly, a lack of preparedness to pay property taxes may leave some borrowers vulnerable to default. Hence, failure to escrow for property taxes is an underwriting practice that may lead to overestimating the borrowers' ability to repay.

Factoring the ability to pay property taxes may not have been standard underwriting practice in subprime lending in light of its origins as a cash-out refinance market. Many borrowers used subprime loans to access existing home equity for consolidating and perhaps reducing overall monthly debt payments, making home improvements, and purchasing durables.[28] Subprime lenders, while catering to this market segment, may not have incorporated property tax escrows because it is not common practice for many cash-out refinances. Nevertheless, escrowing for property taxes was arguably overlooked for those borrowers who leveraged themselves near the limits of their capacity to repay loans. Hence, the proposed QM rule addresses this problem by requiring the incorporation of escrows and other mortgage related payment obligations in the underwriting process.

Low Capital Buffers

Safety and soundness regulation generally requires financial institutions to hold a certain percentage of capital to withstand a surge in loan defaults. If financial institutions have sufficient capital buffers to absorb losses from nonperforming loans, then insolvency and subsequent failures, which imposes economic costs and threatens overall financial stability, are less likely to occur.[29] For bank depository institutions to be considered adequately capitalized, they must have total risk-based capital ratios equal to or greater than 8%.[30] For credit unions to be adequately capitalized, they must have net worth, which is analogous to bank capital ratios, between 6% and 6.99%.[31]

Large complex financial institutions sponsored financial conduits that allowed mortgages to be financed off the balance sheets of supervised banks.[32] In other words, the conduits could issue debt obligations (e.g., short-term commercial paper) to investors without being subject to traditional banking safety and soundness capital requirements given that the mortgages were not held in bank portfolios. Prior to the Dodd-Frank Act, nonbank (nondepository) institutions, as well as the nonbank subsidiaries of bank holding companies, could originate mortgages that would not be subject to regulatory capital requirements. Hence, mortgages could be funded with less capital, and the extent to which this was done arguably reflects overconfidence in the performance of mortgage assets that ultimately stemmed from overconfidence in rising house values.[33] Such lender overconfidence made it possible for borrowers to gain access to credit, which translates into greater type 1 errors. The proposed QM and QRM rules do not directly address issues related to inadequate capital buffers to absorb a sudden rise of delinquencies; however, the Basel Committee on Banking Supervision has called for increased capital buffers for banks[34], and the Dodd-Frank Act also requires minimum capital requirements for banks.[35]

In addition, mortgage financiers or securitizers who purchased mortgages from loan originators, including the GSEs Fannie Mae and Freddie Mac held relatively little capital to support their mortgage lending activities. Prior to conservatorship, the GSEs were classified as adequately capitalized when they met the statutory minimum requirement of 2.5% for loans that they kept in portfolio and only 0.45% for off-balance sheet obligations despite their exposures to credit risk.[36] Given statutory requirements that allowed for highly leveraged and undiversified asset portfolios, the GSEs were as vulnerable as other mortgage borrowers and lenders to a "Minsky moment" or sudden financial downturn in which existing assets cease to generate revenues sufficient to cover financial repayment obligations.[37]

Inadequate Due Diligence in Securitization Pipelines

A mortgage securitization transaction typically involves an originator that sells a mortgage loan to a securitizer, who then issues mortgage-backed securities (MBSs) to investors. The credit risks of the assets used to create structured finance securities are considered opaque by experts and regulators.[38] Despite general documentation about the type of underlying risk exposures and credit ratings, the lack of secondary market trading information (as a result of the infrequent trading of structured finance offerings) and access to loan-level information on the underlying MBS collateral hinder full transparency.

Given the inherent opacity of securitization, all participants of a securitization process might be inclined to perform their own due diligence examinations of the underlying credit risks rather than rely solely upon the assessments of other parties in the pipeline.[39] Investors, however, may have relied too heavily upon credit rating agencies, who may have relied too heavily upon securitizers, who may rely too heavily on mortgage originators to identify the level of risk exposure to borrower repayment problems under deteriorating economic conditions.[40] Consequently, an "incentive misalignment" problem arguably exists when the participants of a securitization pipeline do not all share the incentive to perform due diligence to determine the credit quality of the underlying mortgages.[41] Incentive misalignment problems tend to increase during periods of excessive optimism and foster the proliferation of type 1 errors. Furthermore, inadequate due diligence among securitization participants also reduces the likelihood of detecting deceptive or predatory lending practices. Requiring one or more of the parties in a securitization pipeline to retain "skin-in-the-game," which is the purpose of the propose QRM risk-retention rules, would arguably provide the incentive to perform due diligence examinations.[42]

Implications of QM and QRM Rules on Mortgage Credit Accessibility

The mortgage lending practices that occurred prior to the financial crisis resulted in excessive leveraging that many believe impedes the current economic recovery. The QM rules would increase standards such that borrowers may experience fewer repayment problems after a sudden downturn in economic and financial conditions. The QRM rules, which would require the sharing of any eventual losses associated with nonperforming mortgage loans, would encourage greater due diligence in the underwriting process. The ability to repay and risk-retention measures, therefore, address the proliferation of risky financial practices that are associated with a rise in type 1 lending errors.

Industry experts, however, fear that the QRM standards, which would provide an exemption from risk-retention requirements, might become widely adopted and translate into a sharp increase in type 2 lending errors.[43] Comments on the proposed rules from mortgage industry representatives express a preference to hold loans that satisfy specific (quantitative) measures that can be documented at origination and are less likely to be contested in court or by a regulator.[44] Furthermore, smaller community banks that typically serve as mortgage brokers and sell many of their mortgage originations may choose not to increase their required regulatory capital levels to retain non-QRMs in their portfolios. Consequently, in light of the heighted legal risks, industry representatives also favor harmonization of both the QM and QRM rules into one definition, which may reduce possible incidents of inconsistent interpretations among participants in the securitization pipeline as well as the financial regulators.[45]

The restrictions on points and fees along with the change in the definition of a high-cost mortgage loan would reduce the profitability of "risk-based" pricing or the practice of charging riskier borrowers more to offset their greater levels of default risk. Disadvantaged or weaker borrowers, therefore, would face additional difficulties obtaining mortgage credit. First, the Dodd-Frank Act amended the definition of a high-cost mortgage loan as well as the calculation of points and fees that apply to these loans.[46] A high-cost mortgage loan is defined as one that is greater than $20,000 and has points and fees that exceed 5% of the total loan amount for loans (or exceeds $1000 for loans that are less than or equal to $20,000). Second, the definition of points and fees would include all compensation paid to a loan originator (i.e., origination, underwriting, and broker's fees), prepayment penalties, and upfront mortgage insurance premiums in excess of the amount payable under FHA provisions.[47] Such definition changes increase the likelihood that some low-credit quality borrowers would not meet the QM or QRM standards or hit the trigger that makes high-cost mortgage loans less attractive to originate.[48] Consequently, the proposed standards may result in legal protection provided to creditors when they originate loans to borrowers of lower-default risk as opposed to higher-risk borrowers. Legal protection, however, would arguably be more beneficial to creditors when lending to disadvantaged borrowers.

Hence, while meeting the QRM standards may reduce the type 1 errors associated with allowing financially unqualified borrowers to accumulate large debt levels, the rejection of applicants able to repay non-QRMs may rise. The consequences of type 2 errors may include less credit availability for qualified borrowers, which can impede overall economic recovery. Type 2 errors or forgone lending opportunities are also likely to become more apparent during times when financial and macroeconomic conditions are more favorable toward loan repayment.

The ability to repay and risk-retention rules may lead to a shift of more mortgage credit risk from the financial markets to the federal government. For example, the Federal Housing Administration, which currently has a downpayment requirement of 3.5%, may become a more affordable option should higher downpayment requirements be adopted by the mortgage industry. An increase in FHA business would mean that the federal government would insure a larger share of mortgage originations in the United States. On the other hand, while the GSEs, which securitize a significant share of U.S. mortgages, remain under conservatorship, the QRM downpayment requirements are unlikely to affect borrowers. The QRM standards, therefore, may not necessarily translate into type 2 errors or significant reductions in credit availability as long as the federal government bears the default risk for low downpayment mortgage loans.

End Notes

[1] See Hyman P. Minsky, *The Financial Instability Hypothesis*, The Jerome Levy Economics Institute, Working Paper No. 74, May 1992, and Justin Lahaar, "In Time of Tumult, Obscure Economist Gains Currency: Mr. Minsky Long Argued Markets Were Crisis Prone; His 'Moment' Has Arrived," *Wall Street Journal*, August 18, 2007, at http://online.wsj.com/article/SB118736585456901047.html.

[2] A mortgage securitization transaction involves selling mortgages to a securitizer who pools them and creates a mortgage-backed security. The subsequent payment streams are then sold to various groups of investors. For more information, see CRS Report RS22722, *Securitization and Federal Regulation of Mortgages for Safety and Soundness*, by Edward V. Murphy.

[3] See http://www.federalreserve.gov/newsevents/press/bcreg/20110419a.htm. The rule was published in the *Federal Register* on May 11, 2011. See http://www.gpo.gov/fdsys/pkg/FR-2011-05-11/pdf/2011-9766.pdf. General rulemaking authority for the Truth-in-Lending Act (TILA; P.L. 90-321; 82 Stat. 146), which is implemented under Regulation Z, transfers to the CFPB on July 21, 2011. See CRS Report R41338, *The Dodd-Frank Wall Street Reform and Consumer Protection Act: Title X, The Consumer Financial Protection Bureau*, by David H. Carpenter.

[4] See http://www.consumerfinance.gov/pressreleases/consumer-financial-protection-bureau-seeks-further-comment-on-ability-to-repay-mortgage-rule/ and http://files.consumerfinance.gov/f/201205_cfpb_Ability_to_Repay.pdf.

[5] See CRS Report R41839, *Limitations on the Secretary of the Treasury's Authority to Exercise the Powers of the Bureau of Consumer Financial Protection*, by David H. Carpenter,

Limitations on the Secretary of the Treasury's Authority to Exercise the Powers of the Bureau of Consumer Financial Protection, by David H. Carpenter.

[6] For further description of the *safe harbor* and *rebuttable presumption* legal terms and interpretations, see Board of Governors of the Federal Reserve System, "Regulation Z; Truth in Lending," 76 *Federal Register* 27395-27396, May 11, 2011, at http://www.gpo.gov/fdsys/pkg/FR-2011-05-11/pdf/2011-9766.pdf.

[7] The definition of a higher-priced or high-cost loan is discussed in the "Implications of QM and QRM Rules on Mortgage Credit Accessibility" section of this report.

[8] These requirements apply to nearly all asset classes, including securitizations of credit card loans, automobile loans, commercial real estate loans, and commercial (equipment) loans.

[9] The regulatory agencies were the Office of the Comptroller of the Currency (Department of the U.S. Treasury), the Board of Governors of the Federal Reserve System, the Federal Deposit Insurance Corporation, the Federal Housing Finance Agency, the Securities and Exchange Commission, and the Department of Housing and Urban Development. See http://edocket.access.gpo.gov/2011/pdf/2011-8364.pdf.

[10] Securitizers may retain a 5% "vertical" slice of each payment class or a "horizontal" slice (or the first-loss position) of a mortgage-backed security pool. See the QRM rules at http://www.fdic.gov/news/board/29Marchno2.pdf.

[11] See CRS Report RL34661, *Fannie Mae's and Freddie Mac's Financial Problems*, by N. Eric Weiss.

[12] For complete tables with side-by-side comparisons of Alternatives 1 and 2 of the QM loans as well as QM with QRM loans, see http://www.philadelphiafed.org/bank-resources/publications/consumer-compliance-outlook/outlook-live/2011/052611.pdf and http://www.mbaa.org/files/ResourceCenter/MIRA/MBARiskRetentionRuleSummary.pdf.

[13] For a brief summary of the eligibility criteria for loans to meet the QRM standard, see http://www.fhfa.gov/webfiles/21113/RiskRetentionLawler41211.pdf.

[14] Typically, lenders set specific limits on borrower qualifying ratios or measures of borrower debt burden. The monthly mortgage payment to monthly (before tax) income ratio is known as the front-end ratio, and the monthly total debt payment to monthly (before tax) income ratio is known as the back-end ratio. Prime borrowers, who possess financial characteristics that indicate the ability to meet all scheduled payment obligations on time, typically have front- and back-end ratios that do not exceed 28% and 36%, respectively. The 28% and 36% qualifying ratios are standard for conventional loans, which follow guidelines established by Fannie Mae and Freddie Mac. For loans insured by the Federal Housing Administration (FHA), the front- and back-end ratios are set at 29% and 41%, respectively (see Mortgagee Letters 1989-25, 1997-26, and 2005-16, at http://www.hud.gov/offices/adm/hudclips/letters/mortgagee/).

[15] See U.S. Congress, House Committee on Financial Services, Subcommittee on Capital Markets and Government Sponsored Enterprises, *Statement of Henry V. Cunningham Jr., CMB*, Understanding the Implications and Consequences of the Proposed Rule on Risk Retention, 112th Cong., 1st sess., April 14, 2011, p. 8 at http://www.mortgagebankers.org/files/Advocacy/2011/MBATestimonyonRiskRetention.pdf.

[16] On July 14, 2008, the Federal Reserve issued final rules that prohibit collateral-dependent lending, require documentation of income, require escrowing for taxes, and prohibit other risky underwriting practices that affect higher-priced mortgage loans. The rule requires all lenders to consider borrowers' ability to repay any higher-priced mortgage loan. See http://www.federalreserve.gov/newsevents/press/bcreg/20080714a.htm. The Dodd-Frank Act codified many of these regulations in amendment form.

[17] The term *nonprime* lending may be an accurate characterization of lending that does not occur in traditional conventional or prime mortgage markets, although the term *subprime* has been adopted. Various developments in the mortgage markets contributed to the advance of nonprime lending. Beginning in the 1990s, credit increasingly became available for borrowers with weaker credit. Instead of turning down those loan requests, lenders began

charging higher interest rates to compensate for the additional credit risk. Lending at higher costs relative to prime borrowers became known as subprime lending. In addition, structural trends in mortgage finance (i.e., decrease in the use of mortgage insurance, increase in home equity lending) that occurred during 2001 through 2005 led to fewer borrowers relying upon more traditional mortgage financing mechanisms, such as the FHA Hence, it would be misleading to characterize creditworthy borrowers that relied upon nontraditional mortgage financing arrangements or all nonprime borrowing as subprime. See Rajdeep Sengupta and William R. Emmons, *What is Subprime Lending?* Federal Reserve Bank of St. Louis, Economic Synopses, St. Louis, MO, 2007, http://research.stlouisfed.org/publications/es/07/ES0713.pdf.

[18] See http://ofheo.gov/Default.aspx/webfiles/webfiles/14779/MMNOTE_09-04%5B1%5D.pdf.

[19] P.L. 109-432, the Tax Relief and Health Care Act of 2006, temporarily allowed mortgage insurance premiums paid for a personal residence to be tax deductible as mortgage interest for tax year 2007. P.L. 110-142, the Mortgage Forgiveness Debt Relief Act of 2007, extended that provision through December 31, 2010. See CRS Report RL33025, *Fundamental Tax Reform: Options for the Mortgage Interest Deduction*, by Pamela J. Jackson.

[20] A jumbo loan is defined as one having an amount that exceeds the maximum conforming loan limit. A conforming loan is one that Fannie Mae and Freddie Mac can purchase, which is why conforming loans typically carry lower interest rates than jumbo loans. See the jumbo-conforming mortgage loan rate spreads at http://www.banx.com/images/lazear08_ERP_BanxQuote_Chart_NE-Club-6_550pix.jpg and http://news.mortgagecalculator.org/wp-content/uploads/2010/03/Conforming-Jumbo-mortage-rate-spread.gif.

[21] The private mortgage insurance industry, along with the FHA, saw sharp declines in business as borrowers switched to using secondary mortgages to finance home purchases. See Federal Housing Finance Agency, State of the Private Mortgage Insurance Industry: Implications for the U.S. Mortgage Markets and the Enterprises, Mortgage Market Note09-4, Washington, DC, August 20, 2009, http://ofheo.gov/Default.aspx/webfiles/webfiles/14779/MMNOTE_09-04%5B1%5D.pdf, p. 4 Chart 1; and Table 1: FHA Single Family Activity in the Home-Purchase Market Through March 2010 at http://www.hud.gov/offices/hsg/comp/rpts/fhamktsh/fhamkt_current.pdf.

[22] See Michael LaCour-Little, Eric Rosenblatt, and Vincent Yao, *Follow the Money: A Close Look at Recent Southern California Foreclosures*, Finance Department, California State University—Fullerton, Unpublished manuscript, May2009, at http://www.areuea.org/conferences/papers/download.phtml?id=2133.

[23] See CRS Report RL33775, *Alternative Mortgages: Causes and Policy Implications of Troubled Mortgage Resets in the Subprime and Alt-A Markets*, by Edward V. Murphy.

[24] See Table 2 in CRS Report RS22722, *Securitization and Federal Regulation of Mortgages for Safety and Soundness*, by Edward V. Murphy.

[25] For more information on automated underwriting and its adoption in the mortgage industry, see Robert B. Avery, Raphael Bostic, Paul S. Calem, and Glenn B. Canner, "Credit Risk, Credit Scoring, and the Performance of Home Mortgages," *Federal Reserve Bulletin*, vol. 82, no. 7 (July 1996), pp. 621-648; and Susan Wharton Gates, Vanessa Gail Perry, and Peter M. Zorn, "Automated Underwriting in Mortgage Lending: Good News for the Underserved?" *Housing Policy Debate*, vol. 13, no. 2 (2002), pp. 369-391.

[26] LIBOR stands for the London Interbank Offered Rate, which represents the global benchmark costs (interest rates) that banks and other financial entities pay to borrow unsecured funds from each other. A substantial amount of subprime mortgages were linked to LIBOR. For more information, see http://www.clevelandfed.org/research/commentary/2009/012109.cfm and http://www.marketwatch.com/story/short-term-rates-jump-on-libor-spike-fed-rethinking.

[27] See Darryl E. Getter, "Contributing to the Delinquency of Borrowers," *The Journal of Consumer Affairs*, vol. 37, no. 1 (2003), pp. 86-100.

[28] Home equity lending during this time period was available to prime borrowers. Borrowers with impaired credit had few alternatives if they also wanted to consolidate debt obligations or make home improvements. FHA does not insure home equity loans, and its cash-out refinance program requires borrowers to have an 85% loan-to-value ratio after refinancing.

[29] See CRS Report R40417, *Macroprudential Oversight: Monitoring Systemic Risk in the Financial System*, by Darryl E. Getter.

[30] See table entitled "Risk-Based Capital Groups" at http://www2.fdic.gov/qbp/2011jun/qbp.pdf.

[31] See Statutory Net Worth Categories at http://www.ncua.gov/GenInfo/GuidesManuals/examiners_guide/chapters/chapter17.pdf.

[32] Some critics argue that such off-balance sheet activities would not have been able to occur if banks had not been given permission to participate in a wider variety financial activities. See Thomas M. Hoenig and Charles S. Morris, *Restructuring the Banking System to Improve Safety and Soundness*, Federal Reserve Bank of Kansas City, May 2011, http://www.kansascityfed.org/publicat/speeches/Restructuring-the-Banking-System-05-24-11.pdf. For more information on the supervision of Large Complex Banking Organizations, see Lisa M. DeFerrari and David E. Palmer, "Supervision of Large Complex Banking Organizations," *Federal Reserve Bulletin*, February 2001, pp. 47-57 at http://www.federalreserve.gov/pubs/bulletin/2001/0201lead.pdf.

[33] See Christopher L. Foote and Paul S. Willen, "The Subprime Mortgage Crisis," in *The New Palgrave Dictionary of Economics Online*, eds. Steven N. Durlauf and Lawrence E. Blume, Online Edition ed (Palgrave Macmillan, 2011).

[34] For information about Basel III, see http://www.bis.org/bcbs/basel3.htm.

[35] See P.L. 111-203, Title I, Subtitle C, Section 171 entitled "Leverage and Risk-Based Capital Requirements."

[36] See "Capital Prior to Conservatorship" at http://www.fhfa.gov/Default.aspx?Page=146 and CRS Report R40800, *GSEs and the Government's Role in Housing Finance: Issues for the 112th Congress*, by N. Eric Weiss.

[37] See speech by then Director of the Office of Federal Housing Enterprise Oversight, James B. Lockhart III, at http://www.fhfa.gov/webfiles/1444/AmBar8906speech.pdf.

[38] See Bobby R. Bean, *Enhancing Transparency in the Structured Finance Market*, Division of Supervision and Consumer Protect, Federal Deposit Insurance Corporation, Supervisory Insights, at http://www.fdic.gov/regulations/examinations/supervisory/insights/sisum08/article01_transparency.html.

[39] See Malcolm D. Knight, "Securitisation: Was the Tail Wagging the Dog?," Speech delivered at 33rd Annual Conference of the International Organization of Securities Commissions, Bank for International Settlements, May 2008, http://www.bis.org/speeches/sp080602.htm.

[40] See The Financial Crisis Inquiry Commission, *Final Report of the National Commission of the Causes of the Financial and Economic Crisis in the United States*, January 2011, pp. 157-174, http://www.gpo.gov/fdsys/pkg/GPO-FCIC/pdf/GPO-FCIC.pdf.

[41] Due diligence examination of the thousands of mortgages that would comprise a MBS, however, is costly, which may explain why participants of a securitization pipeline relied upon the due diligence efforts of other participants. For example, the senior investors of a securitization, who are first to receive the generated cash flows, theoretically may not need to perform the same level of due diligence as more junior investors, who are repaid last. In other words, investors choose a particular type of securitization payment structure or purchase other forms of credit enhancements to substitute for more costly due diligence. Hence, characterization of the failure to perform due diligence by all participants of a securitization pipeline as an incentive misalignment problem is still being debated among academics. See Gary Gorton, "Slapped in the Face by the Invisible Hand: Banking and the Panic of 2007," Federal Reserve Bank of Atlanta 2009 Financial Markets Conference: Financial Innovation and Crisis, Atlanta, GA, May 9, 2009, http://www.frbatlanta.org/news/Conferen/09fmc/gorton.pdf.

[42] See John Kiff and Michael Kisser, "A Shot at Regulating Securitization," Regulation of Systemic Risk, A conference sponsored by the Federal Reserve Board and the Journal of Money, Credit, and Banking, Washington, DC, September 9, 2011, http://www.federalreserve.gov/events/conferences/2011/rsr/papers/KiffKisser.pdf.

[43] See Knowledge@Wharton, *Revitalizing the Private Mortgage Market: 'Skin in the Game' and the Consequences for Future Homebuyers*, May 11, 2011, http://knowledge.wharton.upenn.edu/article.cfm?articleid=2775.

[44] For example, see comment letters at http://www.mbaa.org/files/Advocacy/2011/RiskRetentionBrochure.pdf, http://nationalmortgageprofessional.com/sites/default/files/SIFMA_Letter_07_11.pdf, and http://www.americansecuritization.com/uploadedFiles/ASF_Comments_on_Ability_to_Repay_QM_Proposed_Rule_7_22_11.pdf.

[45] See comments by the Securities Industry and Financial Markets Association at http://www.federalreserve.gov/SECRS/2011/July/20110728/R-1417/R-1417_072211_84017_480101591206_1.pdf.

[46] For the definition of a high-cost loan as defined under the 1994 Home Ownership Equity and Protection Act (P.L. 103-325, HOEPA) prior to the Dodd-Frank Act, see CRS Report RL34720, *Reporting Issues Under the Home Mortgage Disclosure Act*, by Darryl E. Getter.

[47] Discounts points associated with lowering the mortgage rate or fees paid to third party settlement service firms would be excluded from the definition of points and fees. For a summary of changes to HOEPA's definitions and requirements, see http://www.freddiemac.com/learn/pdfs/uw/Pred_requirements.pdf.

[48] See comments by the American Securitization Forum on the proposed QM rules at http://www.americansecuritization.com/uploadedFiles/ASF_Comments_on_Ability_to_Repay_QM_Proposed_Rule_7_22_11.pdf.

In: Mortgages: Policies, Proposals and Trends ISBN: 978-1-62257-689-0
Editors: F. Murphy and O. C. Jensen

Chapter 4

ANALYSIS OF THE TAX EXCLUSION FOR CANCELED MORTGAGE DEBT INCOME*

Mark P. Keightley and Erika Lunder

SUMMARY

A home foreclosure, mortgage default, or mortgage modification can have important tax consequences. As lenders and borrowers work to resolve indebtedness issues, some transactions are resulting in cancellation of debt. Mortgage debt cancellation can occur when lenders restructure loans, reducing principal balances, or sell properties, either in advance, or as a result, of foreclosure proceedings. Historically, if a lender forgives or cancels such debt, tax law has treated it as cancellation of debt (COD) income subject to tax. Exceptions have been available for taxpayers who are insolvent or in bankruptcy, among others—these taxpayers may exclude canceled mortgage debt income under existing law.

The Mortgage Forgiveness Debt Relief Act of 2007, P.L. 110-142, signed into law on December 20, 2007, temporarily excludes qualified COD income. Thus, the act allows taxpayers who do not qualify for the existing exceptions to exclude COD income. The provision is effective for debt discharged before January 1, 2010. The Emergency Economic Stabilization Act of 2008, P.L. 110-343, extends the exclusion of COD income to debt discharged before

* This is an edited, reformatted and augmented version of the Congressional Research Service Publication, CRS Report for Congress RL34212, dated May 10, 2012.

January 1, 2013. Most recently, several bills have been introduced in the 112th Congress that would extend the exclusion of COD income again. H.R. 4336 would extend the exclusion through 2013, S. 2250 and H.R. 4202 would extend the exclusion through 2014, and H.R. 4250 and H.R. 4290 would extend the exclusion through 2015.

A rationale for excluding canceled mortgage debt income has focused on minimizing hardship for households in distress. Policymakers have expressed concern that households experiencing hardship and that are in danger of losing their home, presumably as a result of financial distress, should not incur an additional hardship by being taxed on canceled debt income. Some analysts have also drawn a connection between minimizing hardship for individuals and consumer spending; reductions in consumer spending, if significant, can lead to recession.

As efforts to minimize the rate of foreclosure are being made, lenders are, in some cases, renegotiating loans with borrowers to keep them in the home. For some policymakers, the exclusion of canceled mortgage debt income may be a necessary step to ensure that homeowner retention efforts are not thwarted by tax policy.

Opponents of an exclusion for canceled mortgage debt income might argue that the provision would make debt forgiveness more attractive for homeowners, and could encourage homeowners to be less responsible about fulfilling debt obligations.

Mortgage debt cancellation occurs when lenders engage in loss-mitigation solutions that either (1) restructure the loan and reduce the principal balance or (2) sell the property, either in advance, or as a result of foreclosure proceedings.[1] Under current law, the canceled debt (sometimes referred to as discharge of indebtedness) may be income subject to taxation.

The Mortgage Forgiveness Debt Relief Act of 2007, P.L. 110-142, signed into law on December 20, 2007, temporarily excludes qualified COD income. Thus, the act allows taxpayers who do not qualify for the existing exceptions to exclude COD income. The provision is effective for debt discharged before January 1, 2010. The Emergency Economic Stabilization Act of 2008, P.L. 110-343, extends the exclusion of COD income to debt discharged before January 1, 2013. Most recently, several bills have been introduced in the 112th Congress that would extend the exclusion of COD income again. H.R. 4336 would extend the exclusion through 2013, S. 2250 and H.R. 4202 would extend the exclusion through 2014, and H.R. 4250 and H.R. 4290 would extend the exclusion through 2015.

The rationales for this change are to minimize hardship for households in distress and to ensure that non-tax-related homeowner retention efforts are not thwarted by tax policy. Critics argue that the exclusion could encourage homeowners to be less responsible about fulfilling debt obligations.[2] Critics may also argue that owner-occupied housing is sufficiently subsidized even without a COD income exclusion.

This report begins with an overview and analysis of the historical tax treatment of canceled debt income. Next, the changes enacted by P.L. 110-142 and P.L. 110-343 are discussed. A discussion of policy options concludes.

OVERVIEW

For federal income tax purposes, there are two types of income that may arise when an individual's mortgage is fully or partially canceled: cancellation of indebtedness income and gain from the disposition of property.

Cancellation of Indebtedness Income

When all or part of a taxpayer's debt is forgiven, the amount of the canceled debt is ordinarily included in the taxpayer's gross income.[3] This income is typically referred to as cancellation of debt (COD) income. The borrower will realize ordinary income to the extent the canceled debt exceeds the value of any cash or property given to the lender in exchange for cancelling the debt. Lenders report canceled debt to the Internal Revenue Service (IRS) using Form 1099-C, and borrowers must generally include the amount in gross income in the year of discharge.

Exceptions

Historically, there have been several exceptions to the general rule that canceled debt is included in the gross income of the borrower. Section 108 of the Internal Revenue Code (IRC) contains two exceptions that are particularly relevant in the case of canceled home mortgage debt: a borrower may exclude canceled debt from gross income if (1) the debt is discharged in Title 11 bankruptcy or (2) the borrower is insolvent (that is, has liabilities that exceed the fair market value of his or her assets, determined immediately prior to discharge).[4]

In the case of the bankruptcy exception, the debt must be discharged by the court overseeing the bankruptcy proceedings or pursuant to a plan approved by that court.[5] No involvement by a court is necessary for a taxpayer to claim an insolvency exception—the taxpayer calculates his or her assets and liabilities to determine whether he or she is insolvent. For an insolvent taxpayer, the amount of COD income that may be excluded is limited to the amount by which the taxpayer is insolvent.[6]

For both the bankruptcy and insolvency exceptions, a taxpayer who excludes canceled debt must essentially give back some of the benefit of the exclusion. Specifically, the taxpayer must reduce certain beneficial tax attributes, including basis in property, that would otherwise decrease the taxpayer's income or tax liability in future years.[7] The attributes are reduced until the reductions generally account for the excluded amount. As a result of the attribute reduction, the taxpayer may be subject to tax on the excluded COD income in years following the year of discharge—in other words, the tax on the COD income is deferred.

In addition to the IRC § 108 exclusions, there are several other circumstances under which COD income may be excluded. For example, a taxpayer with nonrecourse, as opposed to recourse, debt[8] will not realize COD income.[9] Other examples of when COD income may be excluded from the borrower's income are if the cancellation was intended to be a gift[10] or was the result of a disputed debt.[11]

Gain from the Disposition of Property

When an individual sells property, the excess of the sales price over the original cost plus improvements (adjusted basis) is normally gain subject to tax.[12] If the property was held for more than 12 months, the gain is taxed at a maximum rate of 15% rather than regular income tax rates. If the property was held for less than 12 months, the gain is taxed at regular income tax rates.

In situations involving canceled home mortgage debt, if the lender takes the home in exchange for the debt cancellation, the homeowner realizes gain from the disposition of property in the amount that the property's fair market value (or the amount of outstanding debt, in the case of nonrecourse debt) exceeds the taxpayer's adjusted basis in the property.[13] A taxpayer may have both gain from the disposition of property and COD income.

IRC § 121 provides an exclusion for gain from the sale or disposition of a personal residence. The provision excludes gain of up to $250,000 for single taxpayers and $500,000 for married couples filing joint returns if the taxpayer meets a use test (has used the house as the principal residence for at least two of the last five years) and an ownership test (has owned the house for at least two of the last five years). A taxpayer who does not meet the qualifications may be eligible for a partial exclusion if the home was sold because of a change in employment or health or due to unforeseen circumstances.[14] Additionally, other taxpayers may qualify for special treatment (e.g., members of the armed forces).[15] The exclusion can generally be used every two years.

LEGISLATIVE DEVELOPMENTS

On December 20, 2007, The Mortgage Forgiveness Debt Relief Act of 2007, P.L. 110-142, was signed into law. The act, among other things, excludes discharged qualified residential debt from gross income. Qualified indebtedness is defined as debt, limited to $2 million ($1 million if married filing separately), incurred in acquiring, constructing, or substantially improving the taxpayer's principal residence that is secured by such residence. It also includes refinancing of this debt, to the extent that the refinancing does not exceed the amount of refinanced indebtedness. The taxpayer is required to reduce the basis in the principal residence by the amount of the excluded income. The provision does not apply if the discharge was on account of services performed for the lender or any other factor not directly related to a decline in the residence's value or to the taxpayer's financial condition. The provision applies to debt discharges that are made on or after January 1, 2007, and before January 1, 2010. The provision has been estimated to cost $1.34 billion in reduced tax revenue from FY2008 through FY2017.[16]

On October 3, 2008, the Emergency Economic Stabilization Act of 2008, P.L. 110-343, extended the exclusion described above through the end of 2012. At the time, the extension was estimated to cost $362 million from FY2009 through FY2018.[17]

Most recently, several bills have been introduced in the 112th Congress that would extend the exclusion of COD income again. H.R. 4336 would extend the exclusion through 2013, S. 2250 and H.R. 4202 would extend the exclusion through 2014, and H.R. 4250 and H.R. 4290 would extend the exclusion through 2015.

ANALYSIS

In order to evaluate the policy of including discharged debt as income, it is helpful to understand how it works. According to economic theory, one way of defining income is as the change (over the period in question) in a person's net worth—that is, the change in the value of the person's assets minus the change in their liabilities. By this definition, a forgiven loan is income: a canceled debt reduces a taxpayer's liabilities, and thus increases net worth. In the past, tax law has generally adhered to this concept by providing that if the obligation to repay the lender is forgiven, the amount of loan proceeds that is forgiven is reportable income subject to tax.[18]

This portion of the report provides analysis of the issues associated with the tax treatment of canceled mortgage debt income.

Homeownership Retention or Loss

In some instances, lenders may restructure or rearrange debt, cancel some debt, and allow the homeowner to retain ownership of the home. Then, all other things being equal, the borrower's net worth has increased as liabilities have declined and assets have remained unchanged. Alternatively, homeowners may experience debt cancellation while losing their home, through foreclosure or as a result of voluntarily deeding the property back to the lender. The homeowner no longer has the asset and, to the extent the asset value exceeded liabilities, may be worse off as a result of declining net worth. Additionally, he or she may realize gains or losses, which may make the taxpayer better or worse off as well.

If the taxpayer is not able to exclude the COD income, then the tax consequences of the COD income, assuming equal amounts of canceled debt, are the same regardless of whether the home is retained or lost.

Table 1.Tax Treatment of Canceled Debt Income Assuming No Exclusions Apply

Qualified residential debt	**$200,000**
Loan is renegotiated or property disposed of	**($180,000)**
Remaining balance of debt, which is forgiven	**$20,000**
Tax liability (assume 28% rate) on canceled debt of $20,000	**$5,600**

Source: CRS.

An illustration is shown in **Table 1**. Assuming residential debt of $200,000, a loan restructuring could occur, after which the homeowner owes $180,000 and the lender has agreed to cancel the remaining amount. The discharged debt, $20,000, is income subject to tax if no exclusion applies (e.g., the taxpayer is not insolvent)—if a rate of 28% is assumed, the tax liability is $5,600. Alternatively, the home could have been sold as a result of foreclosure with a sales price of $180,000 along with a lender agreement to cancel the remaining debt. The $20,000 discharge is income and, assuming no exclusion applies and the same tax rate, generates the same tax liability. This is in addition to any taxes the taxpayer may owe on the gain from the sale of the house.

On the other hand, if the taxpayer is able to exclude the COD income, as is temporarily allowed in certain circumstances, then the $20,000 discharge is not included in gross income and the taxpayer does not owe the $5,600 tax liability. As previously mentioned, current law stipulates that the excluded COD income be accounted for through reducing the basis in the residence.

The impact of such basis adjustment could differ, depending on whether the home is retained or lost, in the event that the taxpayer owes taxes when the house is disposed. A taxpayer who retains the house and sells it in a later year, while accounting for the excluded COD income through basis adjustment, is able to defer taxes owed on the disposition until the year of sale.

In contrast, the tax consequences would depend on the timing of the basis adjustment for a taxpayer that loses a home. If basis was required to be reduced in the year following discharge, as under IRC § 1017, then the excluded COD income could not be accounted for because the taxpayer had already disposed of the home. If basis was required to be reduced earlier (e.g., at the time of discharge), then the excluded COD income would be accounted for through basis adjustment and the taxpayer would be worse off than a similarly situated taxpayer who had retained the house and was able to defer taxes until the year of sale.[19]

Equity among Homeowners

An exclusion of income can result in individuals with identical incomes paying different amounts of tax. A standard of fairness frequently invoked by public finance analysts in evaluating tax policy is "horizontal equity"—a standard that is met when persons with identical incomes pay the same amount of tax. Like other exclusions, an exclusion for debt forgiveness violates the standard of horizontal equity. Specifically, a person who has no forgiven debt might pay more taxes than a person who has the same amount of income, a part of which constitutes canceled debt.

An exclusion of income can also reduce the tax system's progressivity—in other words, likely favor upper-income individuals. This is likely to occur because an exclusion of a given amount is more valuable to persons with higher marginal tax rates. This effect is magnified if homeownership is more concentrated among upper income individuals.

At this point, an example may be useful for illustrating the effect income tax exclusions can potentially have on the tax system's progressivity. Consider two individual homeowners, both of whom incur $20,000 in COD income. The tax benefit to the two differs if they are in different tax brackets.[20] The value of the exclusion for a homeowner with lower income, who may be in the 15% income tax bracket, is $3,000, while the value to another homeowner, with higher income in the 28% bracket, is $5,600. Thus, the higher income taxpayer, with presumably greater ability to pay taxes, receives a greater tax benefit than the lower income taxpayer.

Past Enactments

Over the past quarter century, Congress has enacted tax relief for canceled debt in several instances, including assisting Hurricane Katrina victims in 2005 and commercial property owners and farmers during economic downturns in 1986 and 1993. The 2005 legislation was temporary while the others were permanent.

It could be argued that the market conditions that led to the 1986 and 1993 congressional enactments also exist today. Specifically, property values may be declining such that the property no longer supports the debt with which it is encumbered. Currently, the policy issue is posed by residential housing; in 1986, the problem was the business property of farmers; and in 1993, the issue was business real property. In providing the 1993 exclusion, Congress acknowledged it was essentially allowing the taxpayer to defer the income subject to tax because an adjustment to basis was required.[21]

The 1986 exclusion of COD income for farmers may provide the most relevant reference for analysis of the current issues. At the enactment of the exclusion,

> Congress was concerned that pending legislation providing Federal guarantees for lenders participating in farm-loan write-downs would cause some farmers to recognize large amounts of income when farm loans were canceled. As a result, these farmers might be forced to sell their farmland to pay the taxes on the canceled debt. This tax provision was adopted to mitigate that problem.[22]

Consistent with the 1986 enactment, one rationale expressed in 2008, during the consideration of the current proposed exclusion of canceled residential debt income, was the prevention of unintended adverse consequences resulting from foreclosure prevention efforts. Specifically, as lenders are being encouraged to write-down, or work out, loans with distressed borrowers, these efforts could be diminished by the income taxation of canceled debt.

Data

Lenders report canceled debt income to the IRS on Form 1099-C. A copy is also sent to the borrower who is to include the reported amount as income. Form 1099-C is used to report all types of canceled debt, not just residential. As shown in **Table 2**, the number of Forms 1099-C filed rose by 181% from 2007 through 2009. The amount of canceled debt also increased during this time period, from $1.9 billion to $9.1 billion. While specific conclusions about mortgage debt cancellation cannot be drawn from these data, to the extent that debt cancellation represents financial distress, the data suggest that the number of financially distressed taxpayers increased during the recession.

Table 2. Reported Canceled Debt

Tax Year	Number of Forms	Amount of Debt Claimed ($1,000)
2007	271,290	$1,881,848
2008	341,992	$4,192,002
2009	490,846	$9,115,329

Source: U.S. Department of the Treasury, Internal Revenue Service, Statistics of Income Division, Individual Income Tax Returns Publication 1304 (Complete Report), Table 1.4, http://www.irs.gov/taxstats/indtaxstats/article/0,,id=134951,00.html.

POLICY OPTIONS

The changes enacted by P.L. 110-149 and then extended by P.L. 110-343 are temporary and set to expire on January 1, 2013. Congress may choose to let the changes expire, thus returning the treatment of canceled mortgage debt income to its original status. Canceled debt income would then be subject to taxation unless the taxpayer meets a qualified exception (e.g., the taxpayer is insolvent).

If the exclusion on canceled debt income is allowed to expire, improving awareness about the existing exclusions that apply when there is canceled debt, such as for insolvency or bankruptcy, may be an option to pursue. Also, it may be important to ensure that taxpayers know what to do if lenders misreport information on the Form 1099-C, which could make it appear that the taxpayer has canceled debt income that has not actually occurred.

Congress may choose to extend the exclusion of canceled debt income. Additionally, modifications to the exclusion could be made. There are a number of choices with respect to possible modifications. Which modifications, if any, are enacted will depend on the goal of policy makers.

What Kind of Exclusion?

One consideration for Congress is whether an exclusion provision should be temporary or permanent. Early versions of H.R. 3648 (the bill that later became P.L. 110-142) proposed a permanent exclusion, whereas the Administration had suggested the provision should be temporary.[23]

Some argue that current housing market conditions, where there are a large number of homeowners that are "upside down" (the debt owed on the property exceeds the value of the property), warrant a temporary solution for a crisis that is not expected to last. A temporary exclusion of canceled debt income would appear to be consistent with a policy of minimizing adverse consequence associated with loan renegotiations in the short-term.

It could also be argued that the temporary exclusion of residential COD income is preferable because owner-occupied housing is already heavily subsidized even without a COD exclusion. Three principal tax provisions for owner-occupied housing currently exist in the tax code: the deduction for mortgage interest, the exclusion of gain on the sales of homes, and the deduction of state and local real estate taxes, which when combined, result in over $100 billion in lost federal revenue annually.[24] Some economists feel that this preferential tax treatment encourages households to overinvest in housing and less in business investments that might contribute more to increasing the nation's productivity and output.[25]

On the other hand, some analysts might argue that the provision should be permanent. A case could be made that a temporary provision is unfair because there is no difference between an individual experiencing canceled debt income in 2008, when foreclosure rates may be high, relative to three or four years from now, when foreclosure rates may be lower. If the policy purpose is to minimize hardship when taxpayers experience distress, then making the provision permanent would seem consistent with that purpose.

What Types of Canceled Debt?

Several options are possible in determining what type of canceled mortgage debt income may be excluded from taxation. The broadest modification would allow all canceled residential debt to be excluded from income. Currently, only debt associated with the primary (or principal) residence of a taxpayer may be excluded, rather than, for instance, a vacation home or investment property.[26]

Some policy analysts have suggested disallowing second liens as qualified residential debt. Second liens are not directly ineligible for the exclusion, although currently, qualified debt is restricted to include debt incurred in acquiring, constructing, or substantially improving the taxpayer's principal residence.

For some individuals, second liens may be home equity lines of credit, for others, second liens may be debt incurred as part of the purchase of the home. To the extent that home equity lines of credit are used to enhance the home and make capital improvements, it may be consistent with stated policy goals to include this debt as eligible for the exclusion. Yet, home equity lines of credit can also be used to finance consumption, such as vacations or paying off other debt. It may not be consistent with policy goals, some might argue, to include this type of debt in the exclusion.

Congress may also wish to consider changing the limit on the amount of canceled debt that can be excluded from income. P.L. 110-142 imposed a limit of $2 million ($1 million if married filing separate returns). Increasing the limit would likely increase revenue loss associated with the exclusion, while decreasing the limit would have the opposite effect. Decreasing the exclusion limit might also reduce the benefit to upper income taxpayers.

Which Homeowners Should be Eligible?

Policy makers could limit the ability of homeowners to exclude canceled debt income according to certain eligibility requirements.

Ownership Tenure

The exclusion for canceled debt income could be limited to homeowners who meet certain ownership and/or use tests. For example, a homeowner must meet both an ownership and use test in order to claim the exclusion for gain on owner-occupied housing that is available under IRC § 121. The ownership test requires the taxpayer to have owned the house for two of the last five years, while the use test requires the owner to have lived in the house for at least two years out of the last five years. Limiting the exclusion of capital gains in this manner was designed to minimize the possibility that investors, rather than owner-occupants, would be able to exclude capital gains from taxation. Alternatively, it could be argued that tenure is not relevant to the stated policy goals of mortgage debt cancellation.

If an ownership and/or use test were applied to an exclusion of COD income, the number of tax filers eligible to claim the exclusion might be reduced. This reduction in filers may result in lower revenue loss. This policy option would also add complexity to the reporting and filing processes and thus the tax code.

Household Income

Some policy makers have suggested that foreclosure assistance be provided only to households with low and moderate incomes.[27] As with other housing tax incentives, such as the mortgage revenue bond program and the first-time homebuyer tax credit for District of Columbia residents, income levels could be capped and the exclusion made unavailable to those households with income above the ceiling set by the legislation. It would seem that income would be highly correlated with foreclosure, in that those with lower income are experiencing hardship. Regardless of whether this is borne out by the data, it could be argued that household income is not relevant to the stated policy goals for the legislation.

This option could reduce the revenue loss associated with the provision, but would add complexity to the administration and tax filing process, relative to an exclusion without such a restriction.

Should Basis be Adjusted?

As discussed above, current law requires that taxpayers who exclude COD income must essentially give back some of benefit by reducing tax attributes, such as basis in property. Several policy issues arise from this rule. The first is which tax attributes, if any, should be adjusted to account for excluded canceled mortgage debt income. One option is that there be no attribute reduction requirement. Alternatively, homeowners could be required to reduce specified tax attributes that include, but are not limited to, basis in the residence (e.g., taxpayers would be able to reduce basis in property other than the home subject to the discharged mortgage). A third option would be to require basis reduction in the taxpayer's residence. All taxpayers would benefit from the first option by not having to account for the excluded COD income. Whether a taxpayer would prefer the second option over the third one would depend on his or her circumstances (e.g., whether the taxpayer has basis in other property that would have to be reduced in the event of insufficient basis in the residence). The temporary exclusion of COD income enacted by P.L. 110-142 uses the third option—homeowners are required to reduce basis in the principal residence to account for the excluded COD income.

Another issue is when tax attributes should be adjusted. If basis is adjusted, one option could be to make the proposal consistent with current law, under which basis adjustment occurs in the year following discharge of the debt. Alternatively, basis adjustment could occur earlier (e.g., at the time of discharge or exclusion). If basis adjustment occurred in the year after discharge, homeowners losing their home at the time of debt cancellation would have already disposed of the property.

The requirement that a basis adjustment in the amount of cancelled debt suggests a desire by policymakers for homeowners to have to account for the benefit of the cancelled debt. Basis adjustment results in the taxation of cancelled debt income to the extent that gain from the disposition of the home is taxable; however, the timing of the basis adjustment may result in different tax consequences for taxpayers who lose their home.

The exclusion of COD income may result in differential treatment of taxpayers depending on basis adjustment timing, eligibility for exclusion of gain from the disposition of the residence, and homeownership retention. Policymakers may wish to account for that differential treatment, although doing so may add complexity and administrative cost to the proposal relative to its current state.

End Notes

[1] In order to avoid foreclosure proceedings, lenders and homeowners may agree to "short sell" properties or "deed-in-lieu" transactions. In short sales, the property is listed for sale with the lender agreeing to take a reduced payoff on the outstanding loan amount. If the property cannot easily be sold, the homeowner may give the lender the deed to the property in lieu of foreclosure proceedings. The benefit of either option is that the homeowner does not suffer the adverse credit impacts and possible stigma of foreclosure and the lender can clear a non-performing loan without the associated costs of foreclosure, eviction, and property rehabilitation.

[2] Martin Vaughn, "Taxes - Panel Poised To Approve Forgiven Mortgage Debt Bill," Congress Daily, September 26, 2007.

[3] *See* IRC § 61(a)(12); *see also*, U.S. v. Kirby Lumber Co., 284 U.S. 1 (1931)(holding, prior to the IRC explicitly addressing the treatment of COD income, that a taxpayer had realized income from the discharge of a debt).

[4] *See* IRC § 108(a)(1)(A) and (B).

[5] *See* IRC § 108(d)(2).

[6] *See* IRC § 108(a)(3).

[7] *See* IRC § 108(b). The taxpayer reduces basis in property in the order set out by Treasury Regulation § 1.1017-1. Basis reduction occurs in the taxable year following the debt discharge. *See* IRC § 1017(a).

[8] Recourse debt is debt for which the borrower is personally liable if he or she defaults on the loan. Nonrecourse debt is secured by property, and the borrower is not personally liable for the debt; if he or she defaults on the loan, the lender's only remedy is to seize the property.

[9] For more information, *see* U.S. Department of the Treasury, Internal Revenue Service, *Questions and Answers on Home Foreclosure and Debt Cancellation*, available at http://www.irs.gov/newsroom/article/0,,id=174034,00.html.

[10] *See* IRC § 102.

[11] *See* Zarin v. Comm'r, 916 F.2d 110, 115 (3rd Cir. 1990).

[12] *See* IRC §§ 61(a)(3) and 1001.

[13] For more information, *see* U.S. Department of the Treasury, Internal Revenue Service, *Questions and Answers on Home Foreclosure and Debt Cancellation*, available at http://www.irs.gov/newsroom/article/0,,id=174034,00.html.

[14] *See* IRC § 121(c).

[15] *See* IRC § 121(d)(9).

[16] U.S. Congress, Joint Committee on Taxation, *Estimated Revenue Effects of H.R. 3648*, JCX-98-07, October 5, 2007.

[17] U.S. Congress, Joint Committee on Taxation, *Estimated Budget Effects of the Tax Provisions Contained in an Amendment in the Nature of a Substitute to H.R. 1424,* JCX-78-08, October 1, 2008.

[18] This tax treatment applies to many different kinds of debt, such as auto loans and credit cards, in addition to mortgage debt. As mentioned previously, if taxpayers are insolvent or bankrupt, they are fully or partially exempt from taxation on the canceled debt.

[19] The time value of money asserts that the present value of a certain amount of money is greater than the future value of that same amount. Thus, the cost of a tax payment of $5,600 today is more than the same amount paid in the future.

[20] COD income may cause a taxpayer to move to a higher tax bracket.

[21] U.S. Congress, House Committee on the Budget, *Omnibus Budget Reconciliation Act of 1993*, H.Rept. 103-111, May 25, 1993.

[22] U.S. Senate Committee on the Budget, *Tax Expenditures: Compendium of Background Material on Individual Provisions,* S. Prt. 109-072, 109th Cong., 2nd sess., p. 220.

[23] H.R. 3506 and H.R. 1876/S. 1394 also propose a permanent provision.

[24] U.S. Congress, Joint Committee on Taxation, *Estimates of Federal Tax Expenditures for Fiscal Years 2011 to 2015*, JCS-1-12 (Washington: GPO, 2007), p. 36

[25] For an economic analysis of the mortgage interest and property tax deductions, see CRS Report R41596, *The Mortgage Interest and Property Tax Deductions: Analysis and Options*, by Mark P. Keightley.

[26] As mentioned previously, H.R. 1876/S. 1394 limits the exclusion to the residence of the taxpayer, but not the *principal* residence; H.R. 3506 limits the exclusion to the principal residence.

[27] H.R. 3506 proposes a limit of $100,000 for the household income of eligible taxpayers ($200,000 for married taxpayers filing jointly).

In: Mortgages: Policies, Proposals and Trends ISBN: 978-1-62257-689-0
Editors: F. Murphy and O. C. Jensen

Chapter 5

AN ECONOMIC ANALYSIS OF LARGE-SCALE MORTGAGE REFINANCING PROPOSALS: A BRIEF OVERVIEW*

Sean M. Hoskins

The bursting of the housing bubble in 2006 precipitated the December 2007-June 2009 recession and a financial panic in September 2008. With the housing market seen as a locus for many of the economic problems that emerged, some Members of Congress propose intervening in the housing market as a means of improving not only the housing market itself but also the financial sector and the broader economy.

Critics are concerned that further intervention could prolong the housing slump, delay recovery, and affect outcomes based on the government's preferences rather than market forces.

This report provides a brief overview of policy proposals for the large-scale refinancing of mortgages for borrowers shut out of traditional financing methods.

* This is an edited, reformatted and augmented version of the Congressional Research Service Publication, CRS Report for Congress R42577, dated June 25, 2012.

Example of a Mortgage Refinance

- A borrower took out a $200,000 mortgage in 2006 with a 6.5% fixed interest rate to be paid over 30 years. The borrower's monthly payments are about $1,264.
- Part of each monthly payment pays down the principal and the interest. In 2012, the outstanding balance is $184,396.
- By refinancing the remaining $184,396 into a new 30 year loan with a 4% interest rate, the new monthly payments are $880.
- To refinance, the borrower must pay closing costs, which are estimated to be 3% of the outstanding balance, approximately $5,500-$6,000 in this example.[1]
- The borrower lowers the monthly payment by $384 ($1,264 - $880 = $384) and saves over $48,000 over the life of the loan.

Example created by author.

OVERVIEW

With mortgage rates at historic lows, some have proposed expanding an existing large-scale refinancing program, the Home Affordable Refinance Program (HARP),[2] to allow more borrowers to take advantage of low rates. When first introduced in February 2009, the Obama Administration originally estimated that HARP would aid between 4 million and 5 million borrowers. Approximately 1.2 million mortgages have been refinanced through HARP as of March 2012.[3]

In a refinance, a borrower takes out a new home loan and uses it to pay off the previous loan, usually with more favorable terms such as a reduced monthly payment. A borrower can refinance with their original lender or with a new lender. HARP allows some borrowers who are current on their mortgage but have little or no equity in their home to refinance into a new mortgage with a lower interest rate if their mortgage is held by Fannie Mae or Freddie Mac (the government-sponsored enterprises or GSEs). At the end of 2011, more than 20% of mortgagors had negative equity, owing more than their home was worth.[4]

When to Refinance?

Mortgage interest rates are one of the major factors that influence a borrower's decision to refinance. When interest rates fall, refinances typically increase. Borrowers will not refinance every time interest rates fall because there are fixed costs to refinancing. A borrower may save a little each month from having a lower interest rate, but it is only worthwhile to refinance if the amount saved is greater than the closing cost for refinancing. A typical estimate is that interest rates have to fall by 1 to 2 percentage points below a borrower's existing rate for it to be in the borrower's best interest to refinance.[5]

The legislative proposals discussed below aim to expand HARP to aid more borrowers with GSE mortgages that are unable to refinance through traditional methods. In particular, HARP attempts to help borrowers refinance who have little or no equity. If a borrower has little or no equity in the home and house prices fall, then should the borrower default, the financial institution could not recover the full value of its loan by selling the house. Lenders traditionally require borrowers to have at least 20% positive equity in their home to refinance. If a borrower's home is valued at $200,000 and the borrower owes $160,000 or less on the mortgage (loan-to-value ratio or LTV below 80%), then the borrower is potentially eligible to refinance at a bank, credit union, or other avenue.[6] A financial institution that is refinancing a mortgage prefers a borrower to have positive equity in the home to protect the value of the collateral in the event that house prices fall.

The Home Affordable Refinance Program (HARP)

Fannie Mae and Freddie Mac do not originate loans themselves; rather, they buy loans that meet certain criteria from lenders. Through HARP, the GSEs agree to purchase a borrower's new loan if the borrower meets the eligibility criteria. The eligibility criteria for HARP are set by the Federal Housing Finance Agency (FHFA), which serves as the conservator and regulator of the GSEs. The GSEs only refinance a borrower through HARP if the borrower's loan is already guaranteed by the GSEs. A refinance, therefore, does not add additional credit risk (the risk of a borrower defaulting) to the GSEs because they already own the credit risk of the borrower. If a refinance lowers a borrower's monthly payments and makes it less likely that the borrower will default, then a refinance could lower the GSEs' credit risk.

Since the program was announced in February 2009, the eligibility criteria for HARP have changed multiple times, with the most recent major changes occurring in October 2011. HARP currently requires a borrower to

- have a mortgage owned or guaranteed by Fannie Mae or Freddie Mac;
- have a mortgage on a single-family home;
- owe more than 80% of the value of the home on the mortgage;
- be current on mortgage payments with no late payment in the past six months and no more than one late payment in the past 12 months;
- have the ability to make the new payments; and
- have had the mortgage sold to Fannie Mae or Freddie Mac before June 2009.[7]

The October 2011 changes attempted to allow more people to qualify for HARP (the post-October 2011 program is commonly referred to as HARP 2.0).[8] When HARP 2.0 was announced, FHFA projected that the number of HARP refinances would double from the approximately 900,000 that had been performed at the time.[9]

Previously, HARP eligibility was restricted to borrowers with LTV ratios below 125%, but the cap on LTV ratios has been removed under HARP 2.0. The GSEs have also agreed to eliminate or reduce some of the additional fees, called loan level price adjustments,[10] that were charged to borrowers. They will also attempt to reduce closing costs through greater use of automated valuation models in place of property appraisals.

The GSEs are providing incentives to lenders to refinance homeowners by waiving certain representations and warranties the lenders had made on the original loans.

Representations and warranties are assurances that lenders make to Fannie and Freddie about the quality of a loan when they are selling the loan to the GSEs. If it is later determined that the loan does not meet the criteria that the lender claimed the loan met, then the lender may be required to repurchase the loan.[11] By waiving the representations and warranties against the original loan, the GSEs are allowing the lender to re-underwrite the loan to ensure that it meets the agreed upon standards.[12]

POSSIBLE BARRIERS

Experts have identified multiple factors that may be limiting the reach of HARP.[13] One is up-front costs of refinancing. Even after the October 2011 changes, the GSEs still charge loan level price adjustments to some borrowers. Loan level price adjustments, as well as other closing costs associated with getting a mortgage, such as an appraisal,[14] may require more upfront expenses than a borrower can afford. In addition, HARP currently allows for more streamlined refinancing if performed through a borrower's existing servicer rather than through a different servicer. For example, refinances though a different servicer require additional documentation and underwriting.[15] This could potentially reduce competition and increase rates faced by borrowers, preventing some borrowers from participating. Also, HARP is a voluntary program; an eligible borrower needs to find a lender willing to offer them a new loan, which can be a problem given that some have raised questions about the capacity of originators to handle increased refinance applications.[16]

LEGISLATIVE PROPOSALS

Multiple proposals have been introduced in the 112th Congress to mandate greater refinancing of GSE loans.[17] S. 3085, the Responsible Homeowner Refinancing Act of 2012 (frequently referred to as "Menendez-Boxer"), would expand borrower eligibility and streamline the application process for HARP. It targets many of the barriers described above. S. 3085 would change HARP eligibility to include borrowers with more than 20% equity as well as extend the date of HARP eligibility by one year to May 31, 2010.[18] The bill would also prohibit loan level price adjustment fees and other up-front fees and eliminate appraisal costs for borrowers. S. 3085 would attempt to increase the competition among servicers by allowing the same streamlined refinancing process to apply to a different servicer as to a borrower's existing servicer. In addition, the bill would impose penalties on junior lien holders and mortgage insurers if they prevent an eligible borrower from refinancing.

Two other proposals, S. 170, the Helping Responsible Homeowners Act, and H.R. 363, the Housing Opportunity and Mortgage Equity Act of 2011, would also require the GSEs to establish refinancing programs for qualified mortgages that they own or guarantee. For both bills, a qualified mortgage is a first mortgage on a one-to four-family dwelling that is the principal residence of the borrower and is owned or guaranteed by Fannie Mae or Freddie Mac. Both bills would also place certain restrictions on the GSEs' ability to charge additional fees and place a cap on the interest rate that a borrower can be charged. Under both proposals, the refinancing program would expire one year after the enactment of the bills, though S. 170 provides FHFA the option to extend the program.[19]

POTENTIAL IMPACT OF LARGE-SCALE REFINANCING

Housing Market

Mass refinancing proposals for borrowers with negative equity in the homes or "underwater" borrowers generally target borrowers who are current on their mortgages and are therefore not necessarily borrowers in imminent danger of default. A refinancing program that lowers borrowers' monthly payments could impact the housing market by preventing some foreclosures that would otherwise have occurred had the program not been in place. Any potential impact on house prices is likely to be through averted foreclosures. However, because refinancing programs target borrowers who are current, the number of averted foreclosures is likely to be limited.

Several studies have assessed the potential impact of expanding HARP. An analysis of a stylized[20] large-scale refinancing program for GSE loans conducted by the Congressional Budget Office (CBO) estimated that 3.8% of homeowners that refinanced through such a program would in theory have been foreclosed on in the absence of a refinance.[21] Similarly, a study by Glenn Hubbard, Chris Mayer, Alan Boyce, and James Witkin of a refinancing program for GSE loans estimates that 5% of homeowners would lose their home without a refinance.[22] In his testimony before the Senate Committee on Banking, Housing, and Urban Affairs, Mark Zandi,[23] the chief economist and co-founder of Moody's Analytics, estimated that an expanded HARP could result in 2.9 million additional refinances, which would translate to approximately 110,000 averted foreclosures using CBO's assumption.[24] For comparison, RealtyTrac, a publisher of one of the largest databases of foreclosures, estimated that nearly 206,000 foreclosure filings occurred in May 2012.[25]

Consumer Spending

Some have argued that by targeting refinancing proposals to only current borrowers, the primary motivation for mass refinancing is economic stimulus.[26] The magnitude of the potential stimulus depends on the number of borrowers that participate. In his testimony, Zandi also estimated that refinancing would save the average borrower in excess of $2,500 a year.[27] With 2.9 million additional refinances, borrowers' mortgage payments would fall by over $7.3 billion in the first year, according to Zandi's estimates.[28]

Arguably there is a zero-sum component to refinances, with redistribution of income from lenders to borrowers. Although a refinancing increases the amount of disposable income for a borrower, it reduces the potential income for the investor holding the mortgage. Borrowers are more likely to refinance when it is in their best interest, such as when interest rates fall. When a borrower refinances, the remaining amount of principal that is owed is returned to the mortgage holder, requiring the mortgage holder to reinvest at a time when rates are low. However, the gains to borrowers and the losses to investors in mass refinancing may not necessarily be zero-sum.[29] If borrowers spend more domestically of an additional dollar than investors would have spent of the same dollar, then refinancing would increase aggregate spending and support the economic recovery.[30] In addition, a significant percentage of mortgage-backed securities (MBSs) are held by foreign investors and the federal government.[31] Reducing the investment income to those holders of MBSs is unlikely to have a large negative impact on consumer spending in the United States. In analyzing both of these potential channels for stimulus, the Federal Reserve Bank of New York estimates that every dollar that a borrower's monthly payment is reduced by a refinancing would generate nearly 50 cents of additional spending.[32]

Some argue that it is unfair to target economic stimulus through a relatively small number of homeowners who happen to meet certain eligibility criteria.[33] They suggest that if fiscal stimulus policies are implemented, they should have a broader base and not exist within the framework of housing policy.

Financial Sector

Even if the benefits to borrowers of large-scale refinancing are greater than the losses to the mortgage holders, mortgage holders are still taking a loss. Mass refinancing might cause the GSEs, which have approximately $348 billion in MBS holdings, to lose investment income but gain from the reduced likelihood of default, though it is unclear which effect is larger.[34] A large-scale refinancing of GSE MBSs would not only reduce income of large institutional investors like the GSEs, but would also reduce returns to mutual funds and individuals' savings in public and private pension funds, which hold approximately 18.6% of agency MBSs. The Investment Company Institute (ICI), the national association of U.S. investment companies, estimates that 64% of mutual-fund-owning households had annual incomes of less than $100,000 in 2010.[35] However, the value of the MBSs held by investors already factors in prepayment risk, and, some argue, investors have benefited from the "barriers" that are limiting refinances.[36] Others express concern that further intervention now could cause investors to expect the government to intervene again in the future, causing future interest rates for borrowers to rise.[37]

End Notes

[1] For more on closing costs, see The Federal Reserve Board, *A Consumer's Guide to Mortgage Refinancings,* at http://www.federalreserve.gov/pubs/refinancings.

[2] For more on HARP, see CRS Report R40210, *Preserving Homeownership: Foreclosure Prevention Initiatives*, by Katie Jones. HARP is not the only government refinance program. FHA also established the FHA Streamline Refinance Program. However, HARP is the largest of the refinance programs and the subject of several congressional proposals.

[3] See Federal Housing Finance Agency, *Refinance Report March 2012*, at http://www.fhfa.gov/webfiles/23981/ March_2012_Refi_ReportF.pdf.

[4] CoreLogic, "CoreLogic Reports Negative Equity Increases in Q4 2011," press release, March 1, 2012.

[5] See Sumit Agarwal, John C. Driscoll, and David Laibson, "Optimal Mortgage Refinancing: A Closed Form Solution," NBER Working Paper Series, October 2007.

[6] If a borrower has private mortgage insurance, the borrower may be able to refinance if the LTV is above 80%.

[7] See Department of the Treasury, "Home Affordable Refinance Program," at http://www.makinghomeaffordable.gov/.

[8] See Federal Housing Finance Agency, "FHFA, Fannie Mae and Freddie Mac Announce HARP Changes to Reach More Borrowers," at http://www.fhfa.gov/.

[9] See Federal Housing Finance Agency, "FHFA, Fannie Mae and Freddie Mac Announce HARP Changes to Reach More Borrowers," at http://www.fhfa.gov/.

[10] For more on loan level price adjustments, see Fannie Mae, "Loan-Level Price Adjustment (LLPA) Matrix" at https://www.efanniemae.com.

[11] FHFA has filed lawsuits against at least 17 lenders in cases related to put-back claims, which are lawsuits related to potential violations of representations and warranties or other underwriting violations. See Federal Housing Finance Agency, "FHFA Legal Filings," at http://www.fhfa.gov/.

[12] The waiving of certain representations and warranties applies only to refinances through the same servicer and not through different servicers. See Amherst Securities Group LP, *HARP: Program Changes and Their Implications*, October 24, 2011.

[13] The list of barriers to refinancing is not exhaustive but highlights what some experts have identified as major factors in HARP performing below what was expected by the Obama Administration.

[14] As mentioned previously, HARP 2.0 attempts to reduce closing costs through greater use of automated valuation models in place of property appraisals.

[15] See Testimony of Laurie S. Goodman, Senior Managing Director at Amherst Securities Group, in U.S. Congress, Senate Committee on Banking, Housing, and Urban Affairs, *Helping Responsible Homeowners Save Money Through Refinancing* , hearing, 112th Cong., 2nd sess., April 25, 2012.

[16] See Kate Berry, "Bank of America Says It Can't Process All Refinance Applications," *American Banker*, February 8, 2012, at http://www.americanbanker.com.

[17] In addition to the congressional proposals, President Obama has proposed streamlining HARP to allow more borrowers with GSE loans to refinance and allowing some non-GSE borrowers to refinance through a new program to be run by the Federal Housing Administration (FHA). S. 3047 also allows for refinancing of non-GSE mortgages through FHA.

[18] To be eligible, a borrower would have to have the mortgage sold to Fannie Mae or Freddie Mac by May 31, 2010.

[19] S. 170 and H.R. 363 also differ in several ways. For more detail see CRS Report R42480, *Reduce, Refinance, and Rent? The Economic Incentives, Risks, and Ramifications of Housing Market Policy Options*, by Sean M. Hoskins.

[20] CBO did not analyze a specific legislative proposal but analyzed a stylized program that was broadly similar to several proposals.

[21] Mitchell Remy, Deborah Lucas, and Damien Moore, *An Evaluation of Large-Scale Mortgage Refinancing Programs*, Congressional Budget Office, Working Paper 2011-4, September 2011, at http://www.cbo.gov/.

[22] Alan Boyce, Glenn Hubbard, and Chris Mayer et al., *Streamlined Refinancings for up to 14 Million Borrowers*, January 18, 2012, http://www4.gsb.columbia.edu/.

[23] See Testimony of Dr. Mark Zandi, chief economist of Moody's Analytics, in U.S. Congress, Senate Committee on Banking, Housing, and Urban Affairs, *The Responsible Homeowner Refinancing Act of 2012* , hearing, 112th Cong., 2nd sess., May 24, 2012.

[24] In their analysis of a stylized program, CBO also estimated an additional 2.9 million borrowers would refinance. See Mitchell Remy, Deborah Lucas, and Damien Moore, *An Evaluation of Large-Scale Mortgage Refinancing Programs*, Congressional Budget Office, Working Paper 2011-4, September 2011, at http://www.cbo.gov.

[25] RealtyTrac, "U.S. Foreclosure Activity Increases 9 Percent in May," press release, June 11, 2012, at http://www.realtytrac.com/content/foreclosure-market-report/may-2012-us-foreclosure-market-report-7238.

[26] See Testimony of the Honorable Phillip L. Swagel, in U.S. Congress, Senate Committee on Banking, Housing, and Urban Affairs, *State of the Housing Market: Removing Barriers to Economic Recovery*, hearing, 112th Cong., 2nd sess., February 9, 2012.

[27] See Testimony of Dr. Mark Zandi, chief economist of Moody's Analytics, in U.S. Congress, Senate Committee on Banking, Housing, and Urban Affairs, *The Responsible Homeowner Refinancing Act of 2012* , hearing, 112th Cong., 2nd sess., May 24, 2012.

[28] Zandi calculates the $7.3 billion by multiplying the total number of borrowers who would refinance (2.9 million) by the average mortgage balance ($140,000) and the average rate reduction (1.8%).

[29] See Joseph Tracy and Joshua Wright, *Why Mortgage Refinancing Is Not a Zero-Sum Game*, Federal Reserve Bank of New York, January 11, 2012, at http://libertystreeteconomics.newyorkfed.org/.

[30] For more on the spending decisions across income levels, see Karen E. Dynan, Jonathan Skinner, and Stephen P. Zeldes, *Do the Rich Save More?*, Federal Reserve Board, November 2000, at http://www.federalreserve.gov/.

[31] Approximately 30% of GSE MBS are held by foreign investors, the Federal Reserve, and the GSEs. The Federal Reserve System, *Flow of Funds Accounts of the United States*, Fourth Quarter 2011, Table L. 210, at http://www.federalreserve.gov.

[32] See Joseph Tracy and Joshua Wright, *Why Mortgage Refinancing Is Not a Zero-Sum Game*, Federal Reserve Bank of New York, January 11, 2012, at http://libertystreeteconomics.newyorkfed.org.

[33] Testimony of the Honorable Phillip L. Swagel, in U.S. Congress, Senate Committee on Banking, Housing, and Urban Affairs, *State of the Housing Market: Removing Barriers to Economic Recovery*, hearing, 112th Cong., 2nd sess., February 9, 2012.

[34] The Federal Reserve System, *Flow of Funds Accounts of the United States*, Fourth Quarter 2011, Table L. 210, at http://www.federalreserve.gov/releases/z1/Current/z1.pdf.

[35] Investment Company Institute, *Profile of Mutual Fund Shareholders, 2010*, February 2011, p. 105, athttp://www.ici.org/pdf/rpt_11_profiles.pdf.

[36] The potential barriers to refinancing have limited prepayments, allowing investors to earn higher returns than may be expected in the current low interest rate environment. Testimony of Dr. Mark Zandi, chief economist of Moody's Analytics, in U.S. Congress, Senate Committee on Banking, Housing, and Urban Affairs, *The Responsible Homeowner Refinancing Act of 2012*, hearing, 112th Cong., 2nd sess., May 24, 2012.

[37] For a summary of this concern and potential policy options, see Alan Boyce, Glenn Hubbard, and Chris Mayer et al., *Streamlined Refinancings for up to 14 Million Borrowers*, January 18, 2012, http://www4.gsb.columbia.edu/.

In: Mortgages: Policies, Proposals and Trends ISBN: 978-1-62257-689-0
Editors: F. Murphy and O. C. Jensen

Chapter 6

NATIONAL MORTGAGE SERVICING STANDARDS: LEGISLATION IN THE 112TH CONGRESS*

Sean M. Hoskins

SUMMARY

The United States single-family housing market has $10.5 trillion of mortgage debt outstanding. Servicers play an important role in this market. The owner of a mortgage loan or mortgage-backed security typically hires a servicer to act on its behalf. When loans are current, a mortgage servicer collects payments from borrowers and forwards them to the mortgage holders. If the borrower becomes delinquent, a servicer may offer the borrower an option that could allow the borrower to stay in his or her home, or the servicer may pursue foreclosure.

Following high foreclosure rates and recent allegations of abuse, mortgage servicing has attracted attention from Congress. In addition to hearings and congressional investigations, some in Congress have called for national servicing standards. The most comprehensive proposal, S. 824, the Foreclosure Fraud and Homeowner Abuse Prevention Act of 2011 (Senator Sherrod Brown et al.), and its companion bill in the House, H.R. 1783 (Representative Brad Miller et al.), contain provisions intended to protect investors and borrowers from improper servicing

* This is an edited, reformatted and augmented version of Congressional Research Service, Publication No. R42041, dated October 7, 2011.

practices. S. 967, the Regulation of Mortgage Servicing Act of 2011 (Senator Jeff Merkley et al.), includes borrower protections in addition to those offered by S. 824 and H.R. 1783.

The servicing standards proposed in S. 824 and H.R. 1783 include provisions intended to ensure that servicers act in the best interest of investors who hold mortgage loans. The proposals would adjust the servicing compensation structure to better align servicer incentives with the incentives of the mortgage holder. Servicers would also be prohibited from purchasing services offered by their affiliates at inflated costs and passing the costs on to investors. In addition, servicers would be prohibited from choosing a loss mitigation option that would benefit their affiliates at the expense of other investors.

S. 824, H.R. 1783, and S. 967 have three major components for borrower protection. First, the three bills would require servicers to establish a single point of contact with the borrower. The single point of contact would be a case manager who is assigned to each delinquent borrower and would manage communications with the borrower. Second, the three bills would prohibit servicers from dual tracking, which means initiating foreclosure on a borrower while simultaneously pursuing a loan modification. Servicers would instead be required to determine whether the borrower is eligible for an alternative to foreclosure before initiating foreclosure. Third, S. 824 and H.R. 1783 would set minimum experience, education, and training levels for loan modification staff and limit caseload levels for individual employees.

Legislation is not the only avenue to setting servicing standards. Regulatory agencies, such as the Consumer Financial Protection Bureau, the Board of Governors of the Federal Reserve System, and the Federal Deposit Insurance Corporation, may include some or all of the proposed standards in their rules on securitization and qualified residential mortgages pursuant to the Dodd-Frank Wall Street Reform and Consumer Protection Act (P.L. 111-203). Servicing standards could also be adopted through legal settlements between the servicers and the state attorneys general, as well as through enforcement actions taken by federal regulators in response to deficient servicing practices by some banks. If servicing standards are implemented by rule or by settlement agreements, they would apply only to those servicers under the regulators' purview or those who entered into the settlement agreements.

INTRODUCTION

In the United States, outstanding mortgage debt in the single-family housing market amounts to $10.5 trillion.[1] Mortgage servicers play an important role in this market. The owner of a mortgage loan or mortgage-backed security typically hires a servicer to act on its behalf in servicing mortgages. When loans are current, a mortgage servicer collects payments from borrowers and forwards them to the mortgage holders. If the borrower becomes delinquent, the servicer may pursue foreclosure or offer the borrower a workout option that may allow the borrower to stay in his or her home.

Examples of workout options include loan modifications, such as principal balance reductions and interest rate reductions, as well as repayment plans, which allow borrowers to repay the amounts they owe and become current in their mortgage payments. By contrast, mortgage liquidation options result in borrowers losing their homes. For example, in a short sale, the borrower sells the home and uses the proceeds to satisfy the mortgage debt, even if the sale proceeds are less than the amount owed on the mortgage. Foreclosure is similar to a short sale except that it is often involuntary. The home is repossessed and sold by the lien holder. If the sale price does not cover the amount owed, the borrower may have to pay the difference.[2]

Following high foreclosure rates and recent investigations of fraud and abuse, mortgage servicing has attracted attention from Congress. For example, congressional hearings, as well as state and federal investigations, have addressed allegations of "robo-signing," in which a small number of individuals sign a large number of affidavits and other legal documents that mortgage companies submit to courts and other public authorities to execute foreclosures.[3]

To protect borrowers and investors from abuse, some in Congress have called for national servicing standards. The proposed servicing standards include provisions to ensure that servicers act in the best interest of the holders of the mortgage loans and that delinquent borrowers are properly evaluated for loan modifications before foreclosure proceedings are initiated. The most comprehensive bill, S. 824, the Foreclosure Fraud and Homeowner Abuse Prevention Act of 2011 (Senator Sherrod Brown et al.), and its companion bill in the House, H.R. 1783 (Representative Brad Miller et al.), contain provisions to protect investors and borrowers. S. 967, the Regulation of Mortgage Servicing Act of 2011 (Senator Jeff Merkley et al.), also proposes reforms to the servicing industry.

In addition to the legislative proposals, there are other avenues through which servicing standards may be adopted. Some of the regulatory agencies responsible for implementing portions of the Dodd-Frank Wall Street Reform and Consumer Protection Act, such as the Consumer Financial Protection Bureau, the Board of Governors of the Federal Reserve System, and the Federal Deposit Insurance Corporation, are considering including some or all of the proposed standards in their rules on securitization and qualified residential mortgages. Servicing standards could also be adopted through legal settlements between the servicers and state attorney general offices, as well as through enforcement actions taken by federal regulators in response to deficient servicing practices by some banks. However, if servicing standards are implemented by rule or by settlement agreements, the standards would apply only to those servicers under the regulators' purview[4] or those who entered into the settlement agreements. Only legislation enacted by Congress would have universal coverage. Appendix A describes the non-legislative proposals.

This report analyzes the potential misaligned incentives in the servicer-mortgage holder relationship and the servicing standards that attempt to address each concern, the servicerborrower relationship and the relevant servicing provisions, as well as the possible implications of reforming the servicing industry.

ARE SERVICER AND MORTGAGE HOLDER INCENTIVES MISALIGNED?

The Principal-Agent Problem and Mortgage Holders

Some experts argue that servicers face a host of competing incentives, not all of which encourage the servicer to act in the best interest of the loan holder. These incentives could encourage the servicer to pursue foreclosure when the investor would be best served by a loan modification, or they could encourage the servicer to offer a loan modification when the holders would have preferred foreclosure. The tension between what a servicer has incentives to do and what the note holder would prefer is an example of a principal-agent problem.[5] The servicer may make decisions about loans that maximize its income rather than maximize the return for the holders of the loans if the holders give the servicer too much flexibility to act.[6]

A principal-agent problem is unlikely when the servicer holds the loans in its own portfolio because, in this case, the principal is the agent and the interests are aligned from the start. The severity of the principal-agent problem differs for other types of mortgage holding arrangements:[7] investors in private-label securities (PLS)[8] and government-sponsored enterprises (GSEs).[9]

The principal-agent problem may be of most concern for investors in PLS because of their difficulty in effectively monitoring servicers and in structuring servicing contracts, which are called pooling and servicing agreements (PSA).[10] There are several ways in which private investors can monitor servicers. Prior to purchasing a share in a mortgage-backed security, investors can get one measure of the quality of a servicer by looking at rating agencies' evaluations of servicers' performances.[11] Nevertheless, the servicing rights may still be retained by the servicer affiliated with the loan originator[12] rather than shopped around to the best servicer available. This reduces the investors' ability to influence the choice of a servicer. After the servicing rights have been awarded, investors can monitor the servicer through the trustee[13] that is hired by investors to act on their behalf. A trustee may replace the servicer if the servicer violates the PSA by failing to act in the best interest of the investor, but close monitoring of servicers may be costly and difficult. Servicers are not required to transparently report information on loan performance to trustees, and, close monitoring of servicers may not be explicitly stated in the PSA for some trustees.[14] Investors also have limited ability to encourage the trustee to monitor the servicer. Investors may have difficulty organizing their efforts to monitor because they may not know who the other investors are or may wish to free ride on the organizing efforts of other investors.[15] However, just because there are difficulties does not mean that they cannot be overcome. With billions of dollars at stake, investors have organized to file lawsuits against servicers and loan originators.[16]

In addition to facing minimal monitoring, servicers have some flexibility to determine what action to take with delinquent borrowers. To determine which option to pursue on a nonperforming loan, servicers often perform a net present value (NPV) test. In an NPV test, servicers calculate the expected value of multiple loss mitigation and foreclosure options to determine which has the highest benefit for the owner of the loan. Servicers are often required by the loan holder to choose the option that has the highest NPV. Servicers in PLS are generally given discretion[17] in choosing the variables involved in the NPV calculations, which may in theory enable rigging the NPV test to achieve an outcome that increases servicers' income even if better options might exist for investors.[18]

The GSEs have taken steps to address the principal-agent problem. Even before the Home Affordable Modification Program (HAMP),[19] the GSEs offered financial incentives to servicers for performing approved loan modifications. They quantitatively track servicer performance and recognize their top servicers.[20] They also give specific guidelines to servicers for NPV tests.[21] Because the GSEs have assumed an even larger role in the housing finance system since the beginning of the most recent recession, servicers have an incentive to act in the GSEs' best interest in order to attract new business. Through these reputational, contractual, and financial incentives, the GSEs attempt to minimize the principal-agent problem.

During the housing boom of the mid-2000s, PLS gained a larger share of the market. Figure 1 shows the volume of mortgage-backed securities issued by Fannie Mae, Freddie Mac, and private-label investors. Fannie Mae and Freddie Mac have assumed a dominant role since the beginning of the most recent recession.

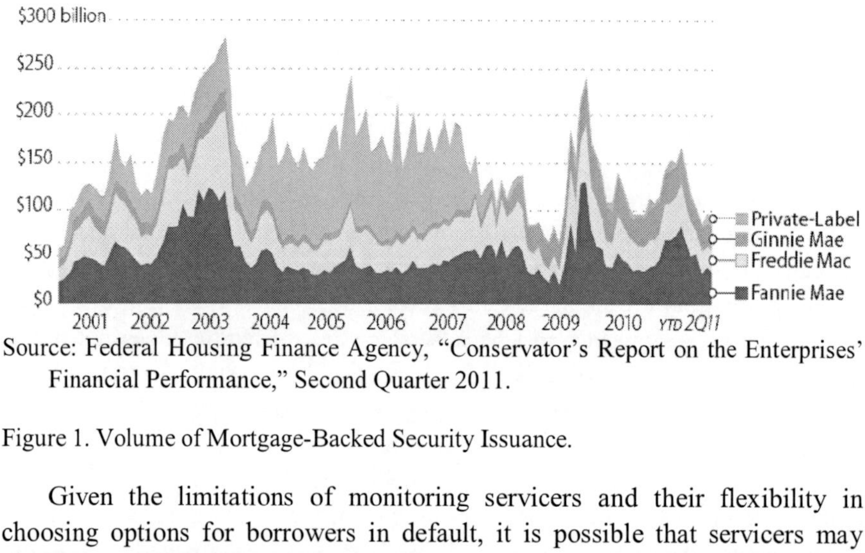

Source: Federal Housing Finance Agency, "Conservator's Report on the Enterprises' Financial Performance," Second Quarter 2011.

Figure 1. Volume of Mortgage-Backed Security Issuance.

Given the limitations of monitoring servicers and their flexibility in choosing options for borrowers in default, it is possible that servicers may choose to maximize their income rather than serve the holders' interests. This is more of a concern for PLS, where the principal-agent problem is strongest, and less of a concern for loans held in servicer's portfolio, where incentives are aligned.

Specific Conflict-of-Interest Situations

The principal-agent problem can be manifested in a variety of conflict-of-interest situations. The conflicts are of concern because they can exacerbate such problems as high foreclosure rates and the breakdown in securitization. The conflicts that arise typically have to do with servicer compensation, servicer affiliation with other entities, and servicer advances. Each is discussed below.

Servicer Compensation

Servicers have five primary sources of compensation. The largest form of compensation is the *servicing fee*. Servicers receive a percentage of the unpaid principal balance on the loans they are servicing. Depending on the type of loan, the fee can range from 25 basis points for a prime fixed-rate loan to 50 basis points for a subprime loan.[22] Second, servicers earn *float income*. Float income is the interest servicers earn by collecting payments from borrowers at the beginning of the month, earning interest on that money, and then forwarding the borrowers' payments at the end of the month. Third, servicers earn *fee income* from the fees that they charge delinquent borrowers. Other sources of fees include property valuation fees, credit report fees, and notary fees.[23] Fourth, servicers may receive *investment income* by retaining an ownership share in the investment that they are servicing. Fifth, servicers may receive *incentive payments* as part of HAMP or other government programs for each borrower that receives a permanent modification.

Some critics believe that this compensation structure leaves servicers unconcerned about maximizing the value of the underlying loan for investors.[24] They argue that servicers are likely to perform a loan workout only if doing so is more profitable for the servicer than foreclosure. This implies that a servicer will only perform a workout if it will earn enough revenue on the reperforming loan before it potentially redefaults to compensate it for the upfront cost of performing the workout. However, critics argue that, under this model, a servicer's decision is independent of the value of the loan and instead depends on the length of time before the loan redefaults and the size of the loan. Servicer compensation does not, therefore, incentivize the servicer to maximize the value of the loan to investors.

S. 824 and H.R. 1783 separate the servicing of borrowers that are current from the servicing of borrowers that are delinquent. Borrowers that are paying as scheduled would be serviced by the traditional primary servicer, whereas borrowers who are at least 60 days delinquent would have their servicing transferred to special servicers that specialize in minimizing losses for investors. The special servicer will be compensated through a fraction of the stream of payments from the entire pool.

The compensation structure for the special servicer is intended to make the servicer indifferent to the type of loss mitigation option and instead encourage it to maximize the NPV for investors. This could better align the interest of the special servicer with the interest of the investors. However, aligning servicer and investor incentives requires addressing both revenue and costs. The legislation addresses servicer compensation issues, but it does not address the costs borne by the parties when defaults occur. A servicer is often reimbursed for foreclosure expenses but not for the added cost of performing a workout option.[25] Some claim that this incentivizes servicers to perform foreclosures. It is unclear if the reforms will address this issue by requiring the same treatment of foreclosure and workout expenses.[26] Failure to address the costs of servicing distressed loans may still leave the incentive alignment issue unresolved.

Affiliate Relationships

Servicers are often affiliated with other entities such as providers of foreclosure services, loan originators, and securitizers. These affiliate relationships may also incentivize servicers to act in ways that are not in the investors' interests. Three types of affiliate relationships that critics cite as sources of potential conflict are described below, together with legislative and other proposed policy options that address each conflict.

First, servicers may be affiliated with organizations that provide foreclosure completion services, such as property preservation companies.[27] The opportunity to earn additional income for an affiliate may make the servicer more likely to choose foreclosure as an option. Even if servicers offer foreclosure services themselves, they are reimbursed on a first-priority basis once the house is liquidated.[28] This gives servicers an incentive to inflate the true cost of providing the additional services at the expense of investors. In other words, the opportunity to earn additional fees may, for decisions that are on the margin between foreclosing and offering a loss mitigation option, incentivize the servicer to choose foreclosure.[29] These additional fees are not required to be broken down in a transparent manner when reported to the trustee, making it difficult for investors to hold servicers accountable.[30]

Overcharging the investor for fees does not necessarily mean that incentives are misaligned with respect to the foreclosure decision. Fees to the servicer and its affiliates are just one component of the NPV test.[31] Foreclosure might still be the best option for the investor even if the investor pays more in fees. Overcharges may not be enough to tip the NPV test in some cases.

S. 824 and H.R. 1783 would limit servicers' ability to charge excessive fees for services that may be sold by an affiliate of the servicer. For example, if a borrower is no longer paying for his or her homeowner's insurance policy, the servicer is required to attempt to keep in place or reinstate the borrower's previous insurance policy. If that cannot be achieved, the servicer must provide force-placed insurance that is of similar cost and coverage as a standard homeowner's insurance policy. This proposal would prevent servicers from purchasing above-market rate insurance from an affiliate and passing the cost on to investors.

Other proposals to limit foreclosure fees have called for servicers' fees to be reasonably related to the cost of actually providing a service and to be disclosed more clearly in monthly statements to investors and borrowers.[32]

Second, servicers may be affiliated with loan originators or securitizers and lead to "representations and warranties" (rep and warrants) conflicts. Often in the case of mortgage-backed securities, the securitizer or loan originator will establish rep and warrants on the underlying loans that make up the pool for the security. A rep and warrants violation occurs when a loan is not of the type or quality that it was alleged to be at the time of the security's issuance.[33] When detected, the securitizer or originator may be required to purchase the loan out of the pool and place the loan on its balance sheet. The trustee is responsible for enforcing rep and warrant violations. Trustees, however, often do not have the loan-level information or ability needed to track violations, but servicers do have that information.[34] Servicers affiliated with the securitizer or originator that would need to repurchase the loan may, therefore, have an incentive to not report the violation. Rep and warrant issues, however, do not necessarily influence the decision of the servicer to offer a delinquent borrower a loss mitigation option or proceed with foreclosure given that this issues does not factor into the NPV test.

To address rep-and-warrant conflicts, some experts have suggested that an independent third party be responsible for protecting investors' interests and be given access to the loan-level information needed to detect rep and warrant violations.[35] The compensation of the third party would be structured to incentivize it to act in the best interest of the investors. However, private investors did, in some instances, hire third-party firms before the downturn in the housing market to perform due diligence on a pool of loans, and this proved to have limited effectiveness.[36] Other suggestions include increasing the penalties for violations beyond just repurchasing the loan.[37]

A third affiliate issue relates to second mortgages. During the housing boom of the mid-2000s, many borrowers took out a second mortgage to help finance the purchase of their home. Servicers of the first lien often retained ownership of the second lien.[38] A conflict of interest may arise if a servicer pursues options for a delinquent borrower that ensures that the second lien will be repaid. For example, a servicer whose affiliate owns the second lien may be less likely to agree to a short sale in which the price offered for the house will not cover the amount owed to the second lien holder even if a short sale may be the best option for the owners of the first lien.[39] The option that benefits the second lien holder may not necessarily benefit the first lien investors.

A recent study has found that borrowers have often continued to pay their second mortgage even if they could not afford to pay their first mortgage.[40] The study used a data sample of 1.4 million borrowers covering nearly all U.S. borrowers that had just one first and second lien. It found that the most important reason that borrowers stayed current on their second lien, which is often a home equity line of credit (HELOC), even if they were delinquent on their first lien mortgage was to maintain access to the credit offered by a HELOC. The study found limited evidence that servicers' conflicts of interest concerning second lien ownership could explain borrowers' behavior.

To address a possible second lien conflict, S. 824 and H.R. 1783 would prohibit a servicer or an affiliate of the servicer from owning a lien that is secured by a property if it is also servicing a different lien on the same property. For example, the servicer could not service the first lien but have its affiliate own the second lien on a home in the pool that it services. Others have put forward less stringent proposals that would require the servicer to disclose its ownership of a second lien and establish a formula to determine how much the subordinate lien should be reduced if the primary lien is also adjusted.[41]

Servicer Advances

When a borrower does not pay the full monthly amount that is due, servicers are often required to advance the principal or interest to investors. Servicers are typically reimbursed for these advances, but do not receive interest on their payments.[42] This gives servicers an incentive to minimize the amount of time that a loan is in default. Although servicers have the option to charge late fees to the borrower, servicers may still lose money on advances because the advances are basically a zero interest loan to investors.[43] This practice may be another reason why servicers might decide not to maximize the NPV of defaults and be concerned about the duration of delinquency or default. Some default periods could be profitable for servicers but other periods could be costly; all periods in which investors do not receive full payment are costly.

Often servicers will only have to advance payments to investors if the servicer thinks the advances are considered recoverable (usually through the sale of the house in foreclosure).[44] The GSEs will also limit advances to four months.[45] In addition, servicers are reimbursed for their advances soon after a loan modification. If reimbursement of advances after a loan modification occurs prior to the reimbursement after a foreclosure, then servicers would have an incentive to not foreclose.[46]

S. 824 and H.R. 1783 would prohibit servicers from advancing the delinquent principal and interest for more than three payment periods unless financing or reimbursement is made available to the servicer.

How Are Borrowers Affected?

Mortgage servicing is not a consumer-facing market. Servicers are hired by investors and, therefore, are ultimately responsible to the investors. Servicers have an incentive to be concerned with the quality of their interaction with borrowers insofar as investors evaluate servicers by their customer service. For example, servicers may have little incentive to respond quickly to borrowers if investors do not value servicers that respond in a timely manner. Typically, borrowers cannot choose to switch servicers the way they can compare and choose goods and services in most markets. Critics say that the absence of this market-force mechanism makes borrowers vulnerable to servicer abuse.[47]

Single Point of Contact and Dual Tracking

S. 967, H.R. 1783, and S. 824 address the absence of a consumer-facing market by requiring servicers to assign a case manager to serve as a single point of contact to each borrower that seeks a loan modification. The case manager would manage communications with the borrower and be available to communicate by telephone and email during business hours. The case manager would also have the authority to decide if the borrower is eligible for a loan modification. If the borrower is deemed ineligible by the case manager, S. 967 would require an independent reviewer to confirm the eligibility status before the borrower is notified. The independent reviewer would be allowed to work for the same servicing company as the primary servicer so long as the reviewer was not under the same immediate supervision as the division that determines loan modifications.

The three bills further address the concerns stemming from the absence of a consumer-facing market by prohibiting dual tracking. Dual tracking occurs when servicers pursue a loss mitigation option while simultaneously initiating the foreclosure process on a borrower. Instead, servicers would be required to determine if the borrower is eligible for a loan modification before initiating foreclosure even if the foreclosure is otherwise authorized under the state's law.

Staffing Requirements

The servicing industry consolidated during the housing boom of the early 2000s. The top five mortgage servicers had a 60% market share by the end of 2009 compared with a 27% share for the top five servicers in 1999.[48] With relatively low delinquency rates, servicers could invest in automating their transaction processing systems and take advantage of economies of scale.[49] Servicers found little incentive to invest as heavily in the equipment and personnel required for loss mitigation. Critics argue that this left servicers understaffed when the delinquency rate spiked later in the decade.[50] **Figure 2** shows how the servicing market consolidated from 2004 to the first quarter of 2010. The rate of servicer consolidation slowed as the delinquency rate increased.

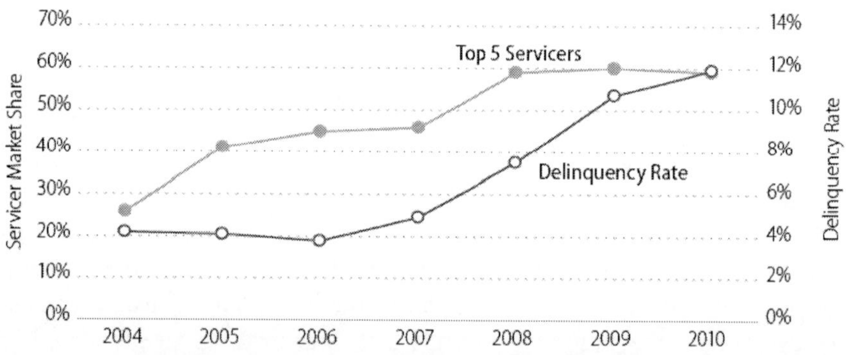

Source: Servicer market share data from Federal Housing Finance Agency, "Servicing Compensation Initiative pursuant to FHFA Directive in Coordination with HUD," February 2011; delinquency rate data from the Federal Reserve Bank of New York, "Quarterly Report on Household Debt and Credit," August 2011.

Notes: The delinquency rate measures the fraction of the total outstanding mortgage balance that is at least 30 days delinquent as of the first quarter of each year.

Figure 2. Servicer Consolidation.

To address concerns about staffing, S. 824 and H.R. 1783 mandate staffing requirements that set minimum experience, education, and training levels for loan modification staff. The legislation also proposes caseload limits for individual employees.

POTENTIAL IMPLICATIONS OF STANDARDS

Table 1 summarizes the issues and the reforms proposed by S. 824, H.R. 1783, and S. 967.

Table 1. Summary of Servicing Standards

Issues	Reform Proposals	S. 824 and H.R. 1783	S. 967
Misalignment due to compensation structure	Require a special servicer for delinquent borrowers	X	
Relationship with provider of foreclosure services	Limitation on fees charged to investors	X	
Rep and warrant conflicts	Third-party reviewer; increased penalty		
Ownership of 2nd lien	Prohibit owning 2nd lien	X	
Servicer advances	Limit servicer advances to three payment periods	X	
Absence of a consumer-facing market	Require a single point of contact; prohibit dual tracking	X	X
Understaffed servicers	Limitations on caseloads and requirements for training, education levels, and experience of staff	X	

Source: Table compiled by CRS.

The servicing standards may align servicers' incentives with investors' interests and protect borrowers from abuse, but could come at the expense of higher interest rates and closing fees for borrowers and lower returns for investors.[51] Just as servicers receive higher compensation for handling subprime mortgages that are more costly to service than prime mortgages, all borrowers could expect rates to increase as servicers would need to be compensated for the added cost of hiring and training more personnel to meet proposed regulations.[52] Servicers may experience reduced revenues as a result of the limitations on the fees servicers can charge and restrictions on ownership of second liens. Hence, borrowers might be required to pay higher rates or closing costs.

In addition, some believe that higher costs for servicers could accelerate the consolidation of the servicing industry and squeeze out community banks.[53] Servicers may satisfy the increased staffing requirements by taking advantage of the economies of scale offered by large call centers and automated transaction processing. If the proposals require that the special servicer for delinquent loans be from a different company than the primary servicer (as opposed to the special servicer being part of the same company as the primary servicer), then the servicing market may further segment into a few large primary servicers and smaller special servicers. If special servicers are also subject to similar regulations about customer service, then they would be subject to the same pressures to consolidate as the primary servicers. If the lack of competition in the servicing industry was one of the factors driving the need for servicing standards, some may ask whether the standards are be self-defeating.

APPENDIX A. NON-LEGISLATIVE APPROACHES

In addition to the legislative proposals, servicing standards may be adopted through other avenues. One channel being considered is the rulemaking associated with the Dodd-Frank Act. Regulatory agencies responsible for implementing portions of the Dodd-Frank Act, including the Consumer Financial Protection Bureau, the Board of Governors of the Federal Reserve System, and the Federal Deposit Insurance Corporation, are considering including some or all of the proposed standards in their rules on securitization and qualified residential mortgages.[54] The Treasury Department, as part of its implementation of HAMP, requires participating servicers to establish a single point of contact.[55]

In addition, the Federal Reserve Board, the Office of the Comptroller of the Currency, and the Office of Thrift Supervision are taking enforcement actions against 14 servicers.[56] When examining the servicers, the agencies found "unsafe or unsound practices and violations of law, which have had an adverse impact on the functioning of the mortgage market."[57] The enforcement actions require servicers to establish a compliance program (subject to regulator approval) that includes some of the reforms already mentioned in this report. For example, servicers will have to improve their staffing and training as well as have a single point of contact to assure that communications are timely during the loan modification and foreclosure processes.[58] The regulatory agencies also plan to impose monetary sanctions.[59] The agencies' enforcement actions may have a significant effect because the 14 servicers represent more than two-thirds of the servicing market.[60] The actions taken by the regulatory agencies do not preclude other federal or state regulatory and law enforcement agencies from taking additional actions. For example, the state attorneys general are in settlement talks with the major mortgage servicers stemming from the investigations into fraud and abuse.[61]

The Federal Housing Finance Agency, which regulates Fannie Mae and Freddie Mac, has directed the GSEs to require their servicers to adopt servicer reforms. Through the Servicing Alignment Initiative, Fannie and Freddie will establish consistent policies and processes for servicing delinquent loans in four areas: borrower contact, delinquency management practices, foreclosure timelines, and loan modifications/foreclosure alternatives.[62] The initiative prohibits dual tracking during the first 120 days of delinquency but does not require (though it does encourage) designating a single point of contact. Because of the large role that Fannie and Freddie play in the housing market,[63] the reforms have the potential to significantly affect the servicing industry. FHFA is also working with the Department of Housing and Urban Development through the Servicing Compensation Initiative to reform the servicing compensation structure for Fannie and Freddie servicers.

If servicing standards are implemented by rule, by settlement agreements, or for Fannie and Freddie servicers, the standards would have a limited reach. Only legislation would have universal coverage.

APPENDIX B. DATA ANALYSIS OF PRINCIPAL-AGENT PROBLEM

Servicers are constrained in their dealings with delinquent borrowers by contractual agreements with the owners of the loans, but the contracts may be vague enough to allow servicers the flexibility to choose the workout option that is in their best interest. Servicers' relationships with affiliates, the requirement to advance payment or interest, and servicers' compensation structures may influence decisions about loss mitigation options. If the option that is selected contrasts with the interest of the investor, then the servicer might profit at the investors' expense. Because incentives influence servicer actions in conflicting ways, economic theory alone is insufficient to determine whether the net effect of servicers' incentives is to offer too many foreclosures, too many loss mitigation workouts, or the wrong type of workout. The potential principal-agent problem is reexamined in this section to see what data trends might suggest.[64] A comparison is presented of how loans are serviced when owned by the servicer versus when loans are serviced for a GSE or PLS. Assuming that a servicer that keeps its loans in portfolio is less likely to have a principal-agent problem, the loans serviced for GSEs should be serviced differently. The differences are expected to be even more exaggerated when comparing loans serviced for PLS to loans held in portfolio due to the stronger principal-agent problem in PLS.

A principal-agent problem may most strongly manifest itself when looking at the data on principal reductions. Servicers are compensated primarily on the unpaid principal balance of the loans they are servicing. Therefore, they have an incentive to not reduce the loan principal if other options are available. Figure B-1 shows the frequency with which principal reductions are performed when loans are held in servicers' portfolios and when serviced for a GSE or for a PLS. The data span the first quarter of 2009 to the first quarter of 2011. For example, of all the loan modifications performed in the fourth quarter of 2009 for loans held in a servicer's portfolio, 27.7% included a principal reduction.

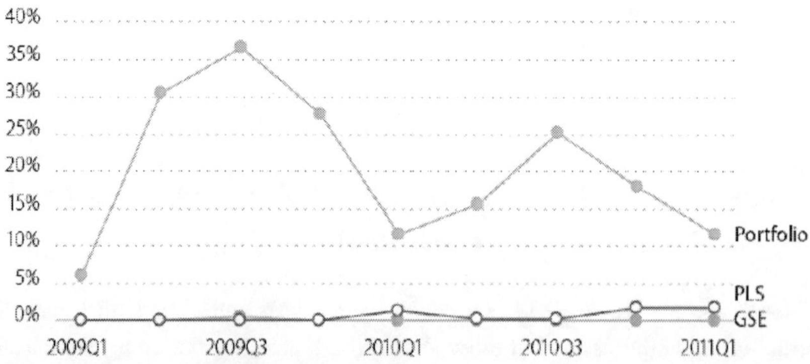

Source: OCC and OTS Mortgage Metrics Report.

Figure B-1. Frequency of Principal Reduction.

Loans held in portfolio saw more principal reductions than those owned by GSEs or PLS. The difference could be attributed to the principal-agent problem. However, alternative hypotheses may also explain the outcome. It is possible that the different mortgage holders own different types of loans.[65] Principal reductions may yield the highest NPV for portfolio loans but not for private investors' or GSEs' delinquent loans. [66] There may also be contractual differences facing servicers for each of the mortgage holders. Fannie and Freddie servicing guidelines do not allow for loan modifications involving principal reduction.[67] Servicers for private investors may also be limited by their pooling and servicing agreements in their ability to offer principal reductions.[68] Servicers for private investors may be less likely to reduce principal because they are concerned about being sued for choosing an option that an investor believes not to be in his or her best interest.[69] Investors may be more familiar with foreclosure or other forms of loan modification and therefore be less likely to question a servicer than if a principal reduction is offered to the borrower.[70]

Other forms of loss mitigation yield similar problems in attempting to isolate the impact of the principal-agent problem. **Figure B-2** shows the frequency with which a principal deferral[71] is used in a loan modification. The use of principal deferral varies over time and the difference between its usage for loans held in portfolio versus loans serviced for GSE and PLS also varies. The amount of that variation that is attributable to the principal-agent problem is not captured in this model because there are too many differences across types of holders.

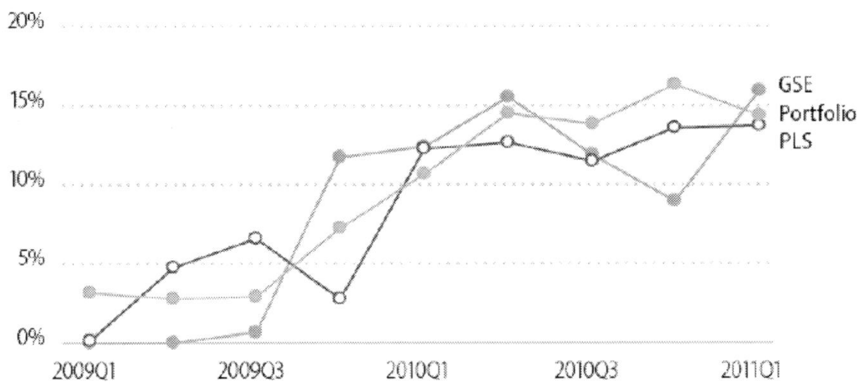

Source: OCC and OTS Mortgage Metrics Report.

Figure B-2. Frequency of Principal Deferral.

These two examples illustrate the difficulty in attempting to isolate the principal-agent problem in the data on loan modifications. The principal-agent problem cannot be measured without loan-level information as well as data on the limitations imposed by the pooling and servicing agreements.[72] Such detailed data are not available. Others have tried to determine if there is a causal link between securitization and increased foreclosures[73] (possibly due to a principal-agent problem), but the results are inconclusive.[74]

End Notes

[1] Board of Governors of the Federal Reserve System, *Household Finance: Mortgage Debt Outstanding*, June 2011, http://www.federalreserve.gov/econresdata/releases /mortoutstand /current.htm.

[2] See CRS Report R41572, *Incentives and Factors Influencing Foreclosure and Other Loss Mitigation Outcomes*, by Darryl E. Getter.

[3] See CRS Report R41491, *"Robo-Signing" and Other Alleged Documentation Problems in Judicial and Nonjudicial Foreclosure Processes*, by David H. Carpenter.

[4] Servicer regulation is often dependent on the servicer's parent company. A servicer may be an affiliate of a larger financial institution and the regulation of the servicer may depend on the regulation of the parent company. For example, if a servicer is affiliated with a bank holding company, it is regulated by the Federal Reserve Board. If the parent company is a national bank, it is regulated by the Office of the Comptroller of the Currency. In addition to federal regulations, servicers may be subject to state regulations. For an overview of U.S. financial regulation, see CRS Report R40249, *Who Regulates Whom? An Overview of U.S. Financial Supervision*, by Mark Jickling and Edward V. Murphy.

[5] Sheila Bair, "Opening Address at Summit on Residential Mortgage Servicing for the 21st Century," Washington, DC, January 19, 2011, http://www.fdic.gov/news/news/speeches /chairman/spjan1911.html.

[6] Office of the Special Inspector General for the Troubled Asset Relief Program, *Quarterly Report to Congress*, October 26, 2010, p. 160, http://www.sigtarp.gov/reports /congress /2010/October2010_Quarterly_Report_to_Congress.pdf.

[7] There are also loans guaranteed by the federal government, but current legislation and academic literature does not focus on those loans so they will not be discussed in this report.

[8] In housing finance, a private-label security is "a mortgage-backed security or other bond created and sold by a company other than a government-sponsored enterprise (GSE). The security often is collateralized by loans that are ineligible for purchase by a GSE," Financial Stability Oversight Council, *2011 Annual Report*, p. 159, http://www.treasury.gov /initiatives/fsoc /Documents/FSOCAR2011.pdf.

[9] A government-sponsored enterprise is a "corporate entity that has a federal charter authorized by law but that is a privately owned financial institution," Financial Stability Oversight Council, *2011 Annual Report*, p. 156, http://www.treasury.gov/initiatives /fsoc/Documents /FSOCAR2011.pdf. For more on Fannie Mae and Freddie Mac, see CRS Report R40800, *GSEs and the Government's Role in Housing Finance: Issues for the 112th Congress*, by N. Eric Weiss.

[10] Pooling and servicing agreements (PSAs) are contracts negotiated between the investors and servicers to help guide the actions of servicers when borrowers are delinquent on their mortgage payments.

[11] Office of the Special Inspector General for the Troubled Asset Relief Program, *Quarterly Report to Congress*, October 26, 2010, p. 160, http://www.sigtarp.gov/reports /congress /2010/ October2010_Quarterly_Report_to_Congress.pdf.

[12] Adam J. Levitin and Tara Twomey, "Mortgage Servicing," *Yale Journal on Regulation*, vol. 28, no. 1 (2011), p. 67.

[13] Working on behalf of the investors, "the trustee's role involves holding transaction cash flows in segregated accounts, notifying investors and rating agencies of covenant breaches and events of default, and managing servicing transfers if the original servicer is no longer able to function as servicer," Moody's, *Moody's Re-examines Trustees' Role in ABS and RMBS*, February 4, 2003, p. 1, http://www.moodys.com.ar/PDF/Research/Trustee's%20Role.pdf.

[14] U.S. Congress, Senate Committee on Banking, Housing, and Urban Affairs, Subcommittee on Housing, Transportation and Community Development, *Testimony of Laurie Goodman, Amherst Securities Group*, 112th Cong., 1st sess., May 12, 2011, p. 6.

[15] Adam J. Levitin and Tara Twomey, "Mortgage Servicing," *Yale Journal on Regulation*, vol. 28, no. 1 (2011), p. 58, 62.

[16] Carrick Mollenkamp, "Banks Pressed on Sour Home Loans," *The Wall Street Journal*, September 23, 2010, http://online.wsj.com/article/SB10001424052748704814204 575508143329644732.html.

[17] A recent white paper that studied the content of subprime securitization contracts found that servicers are often given general guidelines for modifying loans, such as follow customary servicing standards or service the loans as if they were held in your own portfolio. See John P. Hunt, *What Do Subprime Securitization Contracts Actually Say About Loan Modification? Preliminary Results and Implications*, Berkeley Center for Law, Business and the Economy, March 25, 2009, p. 9.

[18] Office of the Special Inspector General for the Troubled Asset Relief Program, *Quarterly Report to Congress*, October 26, 2010, p. 164, http://www.sigtarp.gov/reports /congress /2010/ October2010_Quarterly_Report_to_Congress.pdf.

[19] HAMP is part of the Obama Administration's Making Home Affordable program. HAMP provides financial incentives to participating servicers in order to encourage them to provide loan modifications to eligible troubled borrowers. See CRS Report R40210, *Preserving Homeownership: Foreclosure Prevention Initiatives*, by Katie Jones.

[20] Larry Cordell, Karen Dynan, and Andreas Lehnert et al., *The Incentives of Mortgage Servicers: Myths and Realities*, Federal Reserve Board, Finance and Economics Discussion Series, Working Paper 2008-46, September 8, 2008, p. 20, http://www.federalreserve.gov /pubs/feds/2008/200846/200846pap.pdf.

[21] Ibid., p. 18.

[22] A basis point is 0.01%. For example, a subprime loan with a $200,000 unpaid balance would yield (0.0050*200,000) $1,000 in annual income to the servicer. Servicers are compensated more for subprime loans because those loans often are more costly to service. Subprime borrowers default at a higher rate so servicers spend more to manage those defaults. Larry Cordell, Karen Dynan, and Andreas Lehnert et al., *The Incentives of Mortgage Servicers: Myths and Realities*, Federal Reserve Board, Finance and Economics Discussion Series, Working Paper 2008-46, September 8, 2008, p. 15, http://www.federalreserve.gov/pubs /feds/2008/200846/200846pap.pdf.

[23] Office of the Special Inspector General for the Troubled Asset Relief Program, *Quarterly Report to Congress*, October 26, 2010, p. 161, http://www.sigtarp.gov/reports /congress/2010/ October2010_Quarterly_Report_to_Congress.pdf.

[24] The model that follows is based on Adam J. Levitin and Tara Twomey, "Mortgage Servicing," *Yale Journal on Regulation*, vol. 28, no. 1 (2011), p. 72.

[25] Investors may be reluctant to reimburse servicers for added loss mitigation expenses because pursuing loss mitigation options that maximize the NPV is the expected function of the servicer. Investors may argue that performing appropriate loss mitigation options is what the servicer is already paid to do. See Larry Cordell, Karen Dynan, and Andreas Lehnert et al., *The Incentives of Mortgage Servicers: Myths and Realities*, Federal Reserve Board, Finance and Economics Discussion Series, Working Paper 2008-46, September 8, 2008, p. 19, http://www.federalreserve.gov/pubs/ feds/2008/200846/200846pap.pdf.

[26] It is also unclear what will happen if a delinquent loan reperforms. The special servicer may not have the incentive to make the loan reperform if doing so transfers the servicing rights back to the primary servicer.

[27] U.S. Congress, Senate Committee on Banking, Housing, and Urban Affairs, Subcommittee on Housing, Transportation and Community Development, *Testimony of Laurie Goodman, Amherst Securities Group*, 112th Cong., 1st sess., May 12, 2011, p. 7.

[28] Office of the Special Inspector General for the Troubled Asset Relief Program, *Quarterly Report to Congress*, October 26, 2010, p. 162, http://www.sigtarp.gov/reports /congress /2010/ October2010_Quarterly_Report_to_Congress.pdf.

[29] Fee income is only one source of servicer compensation. Even if the opportunity to earn additional fee income offered the incentive to foreclose, there are also incentives to not foreclose, such as the opportunity to earn additional revenue from the servicing fee (which is dependent on the unpaid principal balance; foreclosing on a home lowers the unpaid principal balance).

[30] U.S. Congress, Senate Committee on Banking, Housing, and Urban Affairs, Subcommittee on Housing, Transportation and Community Development, *Testimony of Laurie Goodman, Amherst Securities Group*, 112th Cong., 1st sess., May 12, 2011, p. 6.

[31] For an example of an NPV test, see Federal Deposit Insurance Corporation, *FDIC Loan Modification Program*, http://www.fdic.gov/consumers/loans/loanmod/FDICLoanMod.pdf.

[32] U.S. Congress, Senate Committee on Banking, Housing, and Urban Affairs, Subcommittee on Housing, Transportation and Community Development, *Testimony of Laurie Goodman, Amherst Securities Group*, 112th Cong., 1st sess., May 12, 2011, p. 6.

[33] Rep-and-warrants violations can occur for many reasons, such as misrepresentations of the income level of the borrower or the occupancy status of the house. U.S. Congress, Senate Committee on Banking, Housing, and Urban Affairs, Subcommittee on Housing, Transportation and Community Development, *Testimony of Laurie Goodman, Amherst Securities Group*, 112th Cong., 1st sess., May 12, 2011, p. 8.

[34] Ibid., p. 8.

[35] Ibid., p. 8.

[36] DBRS, *Review Services for the Secondary Mortgage Market*, August 14, 2007, http://www.dbrs.com/research/213821/dbrs-issues-report-review-services-for-the-secondary -mortgage-market.html.

[37] U.S. Congress, Senate Committee on Banking, Housing, and Urban Affairs, Subcommittee on Housing, Transportation and Community Development, *Testimony of Anthony Sanders*, 112th Cong., 1st sess., May 12, 2011, p. 7.

[38] For example, an executive with Bank of America testified during a congressional hearing that, "of the 10.4 million first liens Bank of America services 15% have a second lien with Bank of America." U.S. Congress, House Committee on Financial Services, *Testimony of*

Barbara Desoer, President, Bank of America Home Loans, 111th Cong., 1st sess., April 13, 2009, p. 6.

[39] U.S. Congress, Senate Committee on Banking, Housing, and Urban Affairs, Subcommittee on Housing, Transportation and Community Development, *Testimony of Laurie Goodman, Amherst Securities Group*, 112th Cong., 1st sess., May 12, 2011, pp. 2-5.

[40] Amherst Mortgage Insight, *Strategic Default and 1st/2nd Lien Payment Priority*, February 17, 2011, p. 15.

[41] Sheila Bair, "Opening Address at Summit on Residential Mortgage Servicing for the 21st Century," Washington, DC, January 19, 2011, http://www.fdic.gov/news/news/speeches /chairman/spjan1911.html.

[42] Servicers may be reimbursed, but often not until the house is sold. Office of the Special Inspector General for the Troubled Asset Relief Program, *Quarterly Report to Congress*, October 26, 2010, p. 162, http://www.sigtarp.gov/ reports/congress/2010/October2010_ Quarterly_Report_to_Congress.pdf.

[43] Diane E. Thompson, *Why Servicers Foreclose When They Should Modify and Other Puzzles of Servicer Behavior: Servicer Compensation and its Consequences*, National Consumer Law Center, October 2009, pp. 23-24.

[44] Ibid., p. 23.

[45] Larry Cordell, Karen Dynan, and Andreas Lehnert et al., *The Incentives of Mortgage Servicers: Myths and Realities*, Federal Reserve Board, Finance and Economics Discussion Series, Working Paper 2008-46, September 8, 2008, p. 16, http://www.federalreserve.gov /pubs/feds/2008/200846/200846pap.pdf.

[46] Mortgage Bankers Association, *Residential Mortgage Servicing for the 21st Century*, White Paper, May 2011, p. 22, http://www.mbaa.org/files/ResourceCenter/ServicingCouncil/ ResidentialServicingforthe21stCenturyWhitePaper.pdf.

[47] U.S. Congress, House Committee on Financial Services, Subcommittee on Financial Institutions and Consumer Credit and Subcommittee on Oversight and Investigations, *Testimony of Raj Date*, 112th Cong., 1st sess., July 7, 2011, p. 2.

[48] Office of the Special Inspector General for the Troubled Asset Relief Program, *Quarterly Report to Congress*, October 26, 2010, p. 163, http://www.sigtarp.gov/reports /congress/ 2010/ October2010_Quarterly_Report_to_Congress.pdf.

[49] A 2007 study found that mega servicers can service performing loans at a monthly cost of approximately $4/loan, large servicers at a cost of $6/loan, and small/medium servicers at $7/loan. See Federal Housing Finance Agency, *Servicing Compensation Initiative pursuant to FHFA Directive in Coordination with HUD*, February 2011, p. 8, http://www.fhfa.gov/ webfiles/19719/FHFA_Servicing_Initiative_-_Background_and_Issues_2011-02-14_3pm_FINAL.pdf.

[50] See the discussion of the enforcement actions taken by the regulatory agencies in Appendix A.

[51] Adam J. Levitin and Tara Twomey, "Mortgage Servicing," *Yale Journal on Regulation*, vol. 28, no. 1 (2011), p. 89.

[52] For more on the potential costs of requiring a single point of contact and prohibiting dual tracking, see Mortgage Bankers Association, *Residential Mortgage Servicing for the 21st Century*, White Paper, May 2011, pp. 23-24, http://www.mbaa.org/files/Resource Center/ServicingCouncil/ResidentialServicingforthe21stCenturyWhitePaper.pdf.

[53] U.S. Congress, Senate Committee on Banking, Housing, and Urban Affairs, *Testimony of Jack Hopkins, President and CEO of CorTrust Bank*, 112th Cong., 1st sess., August 2, 2011.

[54] Comptroller of the Currency, Federal Reserve System, Federal Deposit Insurance Corporation, Federal Housing Finance Agency, Securities and Exchange Commission, Housing and

Urban Development Department, "Credit Risk Retention," 76 *Federal Register* 24127, April 29, 2011.

[55] U.S. Department of the Treasury, *Supplemental Directive 11-04: Single Point of Contact for Borrower Assistance*, May 18, 2011, https://www.hmpadmin.com/portal/news/docs/2011 /hampupdate051811.pdf.

[56] The 14 servicers are Ally Bank/ GMAC, Aurora Bank, Bank of America, Citibank, EverBank, HSBC, JPMorgan Chase, MetLife, OneWest, PNC, Sovereign Bank, SunTrust, U.S. Bank, and Wells Fargo.

[57] Federal Reserve System, Office of the Comptroller of the Currency, Office of Thrift Supervision, *Interagency Review of Foreclosure Policies and Practices*, April 2011, p. 13, http://www.occ.gov/news-issuances/news-releases/ 2011/nr-occ-2011-47a.pdf.

[58] Federal Reserve System, Office of the Comptroller of the Currency, Office of Thrift Supervision, *Interagency Review of Foreclosure Policies and Practices*, April 2011, p. 13, http://www.occ.gov/news-issuances/news-releases/ 2011/nr-occ-2011-47a.pdf.

[59] The Federal Reserve System, *Press Release*, April 13, 2011, http://www.federalreserve.gov /newsevents/press/enforcement/20110413a.htm.

[60] Federal Reserve System, Office of the Comptroller of the Currency, Office of Thrift Supervision, *Interagency Review of Foreclosure Policies and Practices*, April 2011, p. 3, http://www.occ.gov/news-issuances/news-releases/ 2011/nr-occ-2011-47a.pdf.

[61] Brady Dennis, "State attorneys general tackle mortgage servicing," *Washington Post*, March 17, 2011, http://www.washingtonpost.com/business/economy/state-attorneys-general-tackle-mortgage-servicing/2011/03/17/ ABGmNCn_story.html.

[62] Federal Housing Finance Agency, *Frequently Asked Questions- Servicing Alignment Initiative*, April 28, 2011, p. 1, http://www.fhfa.gov/webfiles/21191/FAQs42811Final.pdf.

[63] See **Figure 1**.

[64] The data is taken from the OCC and OTS Mortgage Metrics Reports, which can be accessed at http://www.ots.treas.gov/?p=Mortgage%20Metrics%20Report. The reports contain data from eight national banks (Bank of America, JPMorgan Chase, Citibank, HSBC, MetLife, PNC, U.S. Bank, and Wells Fargo) and one thrift (OneWest Bank). Collectively, the nine institutions represent 63% of all first-lien residential mortgages outstanding in the United States. For more on the data, see *OCC/OTS Mortgage Metrics Loan-Level Data Collection: Field Definitions*, April 20, 2009, http://www.occ.gov/publications/publications-by-type/other-publications-reports/ mortgage-metrics-q2-2009/loan-level-data-field-defin-q2-2009.pdf.

[65] Loans held in servicers' portfolios reportedly tend to be nonconforming loans with increased risk characteristics and geographic concentration in weaker real estate markets, whereas GSEs have a greater percentage of prime loans. No background is given on PLS loans. Office of Comptroller of the Currency, Office of Thrift Supervision, *OCC and OTS Mortgage Metrics Report*, First Quarter 2011, p. 14,17, http://www.ots.treas.gov /_files/ 490078.pdf.

[66] For an analysis of why principal reduction may not be pursued, see Chris Foote, Kris Gerardi, and Paul Willen, *The seductive but flawed logic of principal reduction*, Federal Reserve Bank of Atlanta, March 9, 2011, http://realestateresearch.frbatlanta.org/rer/2011/03 /seductive-but-flawed-logic-of-principal-reduction.html.

[67] Office of Comptroller of the Currency, Office of Thrift Supervision, *OCC and OTS Mortgage Metrics Report*, First Quarter 2011, p. 27, http://www.ots.treas.gov/_files/490078.pdf; see Fannie Mae, *Fannie Mae Single Family 2011 Servicing Guide*, June 10, 2011, pp. 706-67, https://www.efanniemae.com/sf/guides/ssg/svcg/svc061011.pdf.

[68] One study noted that PSA bans on mortgage modification are rare, but the analysis is based on a relatively small sample of securitizations. See John P. Hunt, *What Do Subprime Securitization Contracts Actually Say About Loan Modification? Preliminary Results and Implications*, Berkeley Center for Law, Business and the Economy, March 25, 2009, pp.7-8.

[69] Larry Cordell, Karen Dynan, and Andreas Lehnert, et al., *The Incentives of Mortgage Servicers: Myths and Realities*, Federal Reserve Board, Washington, D.C., Working Paper 2008-46 of the Finance and Economics Discussion Series, September 8, 2008, p. 23, http://www.federalreserve.gov/pubs/feds/2008/200846/200846pap.pdf.

[70] However, there have been few instances of investor litigation in response to a servicer's loan modification decision. See Diane E. Thompson, *Why Servicers Foreclose When They Should Modify and Other Puzzles of Servicer Behavior: Servicer Compensation and its Consequences*, National Consumer Law Center, October 2009, p. 8.

[71] Principal deferral modifications are modifications "that remove a portion of the principal from the amount used to calculate monthly principal and interest payments for a set period. The deferred amount becomes due at the end of the loan term." In a principal reduction modification, a portion of the principal amounted is permanently forgiven. Office of Comptroller of the Currency, Office of Thrift Supervision, *OCC and OTS Mortgage Metrics Report*, First Quarter 2011, p. 10, http://www.ots.treas.gov/_files/490078.pdf.

[72] Regulators have reviewed servicers' foreclosure activities, but have not have not focused extensively on servicers' loan modification processes. See Federal Reserve System, Office of the Comptroller of the Currency, Office of Thrift Supervision, *Interagency Review of Foreclosure Policies and Practices*, April 2011, p. 2, http://www.occ.gov/news-issuances/news-releases/2011/nr-occ-2011-47a.pdf.

[73] See Tomasz Piskorski, Amit Seru, and Vikrant Vig, *Securitization and Distressed Loan Renegotiation: Evidence from the Subprime Mortgage Crisis*, Chicago Booth School of Business Research Paper No. 09-02 , April 15, 2010.

[74] See Manuel Adelino, Kristopher Gerardi, and Paul S. Willen, *What Explains Differences in Foreclosure Rates? A Response to Piskorski, Seru, and Vig*, Federal Reserve Bank of Boston, Working Paper 10-2, http://www.bos.frb.org/ economic/wp/wp2010/wp1002.htm.

In: Mortgages: Policies, Proposals and Trends ISBN: 978-1-62257-689-0
Editors: F. Murphy and O. C. Jensen

Chapter 7

COMMERCIAL AND RESIDENTIAL MORTGAGES*

N. Eric Weiss

SUMMARY

Government regulators, investment bankers, and others have testified at congressional hearings that a significant volume of commercial mortgages could default, causing major losses for commercial banks, savings institutions, life insurance companies, government-sponsored enterprises (GSEs), and issuers of commercial mortgage-backed securities (CMBS). These losses, coming after losses on residential mortgages and other loans, have the potential to further reduce the capital of lenders, perhaps leading to additional bank closings. The closings may result in Federal Deposit Insurance Company (FDIC) expenditures to honor its insurance on deposits. The FDIC could act in ways that would protect uninsured deposits, but this would cost the government additional money.

Widespread evidence shows that commercial mortgage defaults and losses have been unusually high. More recently, it appears that there is some recovery, but this recovery varies across the nation and across various types of commercial mortgages.

---

* This is an edited, reformatted and augmented version of the Congressional Research Service Publication, CRS Report for Congress R41046, dated October 13, 2011.

According to recent statistics, there are $3.1 trillion in commercial mortgages outstanding with $500 billion maturing in the next few years. One investment banker has testified to the Joint Economic Committee that losses for one type of commercial mortgage financing (commercial mortgage-backed securities) could reach 9%-12% or $65 billion to $90 billion; in the real estate bust of the early 1990s, the worst performing groups of mortgages had loss rates of around 10%. This suggests that commercial mortgage losses could be comparable to those in the early 1990s.

Some commercial real estate lenders will be more affected by mortgage losses than others. For example, FDIC statistics suggest that small banks (those with less than $1 billion in assets) are relatively more exposed to commercial real estate loans and losses than are large banks.

Treasury Secretary Timothy Geithner has expressed the belief that the commercial mortgage losses can be handled with the tools available.

This report discusses the severity of the problems that the commercial mortgage defaults may cause the financial system, the tools available to reduce such problems, and some areas for possible congressional oversight.

CONCERN OVER COMMERCIAL AND MULTIFAMILY REAL ESTATE FINANCE

Elevated delinquency and foreclosure rates for residential mortgages have led some to worry that mortgages for commercial real estate (CRE) could be in a similar situation and perhaps face even more difficulties in the future.[1] Notably, in January 2010, a large multifamily project in New York City (Stuyvesant Town and Peter Cooper Village) purchased for $5.4 billion defaulted on $4.4 billion in mortgages.[2] The owners of Stuyvesant Town and Peter Cooper Village agreed to turn the properties over to the lenders.[3] More recently, there have been media reports of a slowing of the decline or a growing recovery in commercial real estate.[4]

In 2010, Treasury Secretary Timothy Geithner said that commercial real estate was "a problem the economy can manage through even though it's going to be still exceptionally difficult."[5] More recently he testified

> While substantial progress has been made, significant challenges remain. In the banking system, charge-offs for residential, consumer, and commercial loans are still elevated, and the FDIC projects that the rate of bank failures will remain high.[6]

A best case scenario builds on a strengthening economy, minimal commercial real estate foreclosures, and lenders having sufficient reserves to absorb whatever losses occur. A more pessimistic scenario looks at the need to refinance maturing commercial mortgages at a time when commercial property values have declined along with the ability to refinance maturing mortgages, leading to defaults, foreclosures, and large losses for a financial sector with reduced loss reserves to absorb such losses.

Hoping that the economy recovers, borrowers have approached lenders seeking loan modifications and extensions. Many commercial mortgages contain provisions allowing the term of the loan to be extended. There are at least three types of impediments to modifying the mortgages in both residential and commercial mortgage-backed securities (CMBS), which are pools of commercial real estate mortgages that are combined and sold to investors: (1) tax considerations for mortgages pooled into mortgage-backed securities (MBS) in a tax-favored pass-through structure known as real estate mortgage investments conduits (REMICs), (2) the pooling and servicing agreements governing MBS, and (3) regulations that financial intermediaries must follow.

Fitch Ratings has forecast that "commercial property performance will slowly stabilize and report slight improvements for 2011. The recovery of commercial properties tends to lag the recovery of the U.S. economy. Recovery will continue to be influenced by factors such as unemployment and consumer spending."[7]

According to the Mortgage Bankers' Association,[8] delinquency rates on commercial and multifamily mortgages for different categories of lenders were mixed. (This is based on first quarter 2011 data, which is the most recently available data.)

Past Government Intervention

The Administration has taken a number of steps to reduce the adverse impact of commercial real estate on the economy, and Congress might wish to exercise oversight on some of them. As is further discussed below, the Administration has modified tax regulations, used Troubled Asset Relief Program (TARP) funds, and used the Term Asset-Backed Securities Loan Fund (TALF) to provide liquidity and relief to commercial mortgage lenders.

Treasury and the Internal Revenue Service modified regulations to encourage some commercial mortgage modification for loans contained in

CMBS.[9] As part of the ongoing legislative consideration of securitization, policy issues affecting CMBS include Treasury's TARP, the Fed's TALF, securitization reforms, fair value accounting, securitization accounting, credit rating agencies, taxation, and covered bonds.

Risk to Government and Taxpayers

There are at least three channels through which the federal government and taxpayers could be exposed to losses on commercial real estate:

- First, insured depositories—especially small banks—have significant exposure to commercial mortgages. The FDIC could be forced to intervene to honor its insurance of deposits. The FDIC could act in ways that would protect uninsured deposits, but this would cost the government additional money. The insurance is funded by assessments on insured deposits, but if the funds were to be inadequate, the FDIC could ask Congress for special appropriations.
- Second, the Federal Housing Administration (FHA) guarantees mortgages on multifamily housing, assisted-living facilities, nursing homes, and hospitals. If property owners fail to make their payments, FHA would be required to honor its guarantees to the lenders. Potentially, the FHA insurance fund could be exhausted, and FHA could ask Congress for additional funding.
- Third, Fannie Mae and Freddie Mac, which have commitments from the federal government to purchase however much preferred stock is necessary to keep each of these government-sponsored enterprises (GSEs) solvent through 2012 and a limited commitment beyond 2012, have guaranteed multifamily mortgages. If these mortgages are foreclosed upon, the GSEs most likely would lose money; and to keep the GSEs solvent, Treasury could be required to purchase additional preferred stock and would issue debt (subject to the debt ceiling) to purchase the stock.

None of these three events is certain, and the Administration has limited discretion to reduce the direct cost to taxpayers. The FDIC has proposed increasing the rate charged most banks for insurance to 1.35% of total assets from 1.15% on insured deposits.[10] FHA could also increase its insurance fees, but unlike the FDIC, the FHA would need congressional approval to do this.

The conservatorship agreements between Treasury and Fannie Mae, and between Treasury and Freddie Mac are legal contracts that can be enforced by the courts, so there is little or no discretion in this case. Fannie Mae and Freddie Mac are experiencing relatively small increases in multifamily default rates compared with other lenders.[11] This could result in relatively small losses and relatively small cost to the government.

Securitization—packaging commercial mortgages into negotiable securities—has spread the rewards and risks of CMBS internationally. Losses from commercial real estate are not confined to the United States, and trouble with overseas real estate can expose U.S. investors to losses. For example, commercial real estate price declines in Greece could cause losses for lenders, which could affect some U.S. investors.

LEGISLATIVE ISSUES

One of the main roles for Congress may be oversight, although legislation could be introduced with or without hearings.

Some Members of Congress circulated "Dear Colleague" letters asking the Administration to support the commercial real estate mortgage market through instructions from bank regulators in Washington, DC, to field staff and by encouraging regulated lenders to provide refinancing when this action is prudent. A group of financial regulators, including the FDIC, issued a policy statement on prudent commercial real estate loan workouts.[12]

As part of its oversight of banking and securities regulation, Congress might wish to consider oversight hearings into the risks to the nation's economy created by some of the commercial real estate practices and current efforts at loss mitigation by the private sector and the federal government. The regulatory agencies could include in their examinations an inspection of the plans that lenders have for commercial real estate price declines.

In testimony before the Congressional Financial Crisis Inquiry Commission, Kenneth T. Rosen, chairman of the Fisher Center for Real Estate and Urban Economics at the University of California, Berkeley, recommended that future commercial mortgages be limited to no more than 75% of a property's value and that this be reduced in boom times; currently, lenders determine the maximum percentage they will lend on commercial property.[13]

Accounting rules require many lenders and investors to adjust their balance sheets to reflect actual current values ("mark-to-market"). Marking CMBS to market is frequently difficult because there is seldom an active market in the various tranches of a CMBS, and the value of the underlying properties could be difficult to determine because many commercial properties are unique.[14] The result is that financial statements to investors are likely to contain a great deal of uncertainty. Congress might wish to hold hearings on the impact of mark-to-market on commercial real estate. Opponents of mark-to-market argue that it can force companies to respond to short-term price changes that have no long-term impact, especially for assets that companies do not intend to sell before maturity. Mark-to-market supporters argue that it provides the best estimate of the current values of assets and that companies might decide to sell assets that they originally intended to hold to maturity.

Treasury's TARP was authorized by the Emergency Economic Stabilization Act of 2008 (P.L. 110-343) to allow the government to purchase certain assets to stabilize the financial system.[15] It expired in October 2010. Treasury used TARP to create a variety of programs, some of which were used to provide support for lenders that have lost capital because of commercial real estate loan losses.

The Fed's TALF had provisions to provide liquidity to the CMBS market.[16] TALF loans required good collateral (such as some CMBS). As of the end of August 2011, the Fed reported that it had $3 billion outstanding in TALF CMBS-backed loans and $9 billion in other loans.[17]

The State of the Commercial Real Estate Market

At the end of the second quarter of 2011, commercial real estate mortgages totaled $3,113.2 billion compared with $13,642.6 billion in total mortgages.[18] CRE mortgages are concentrated in sectors that presently are financially weak. **Table 1** lists sources of commercial mortgages. Some of the largest sources such as commercial banks (44.92%) and savings institutions (5.55%) were in financial distress.

Commercial lending has slowed. Commercial mortgages outstanding have declined from a peak of $3,480.1 billion at the end of 2008 to $3,113.1 billion at the end of the second quarter of 2011. There has not been a year-on-year decline in commercial mortgages outstanding since 1994. This decline was concentrated in commercial banks, CMBS, and "other" sectors.

Table 1. Sources of Commercial Mortgages Second Quarter, 2011

Source	Volume ($ billions)	Percentage of Total Volume
State and local governments, excluding employee retirement funds	$88.50	2.84%
Federal government	80.10	2.57
Commercial banking	1,354.30	43.50
Savings institutions	177.10	5.69
Life insurance companies	303.90	9.76
Government-sponsored enterprises	254.60	8.18
Agency-and GSE-backed mortgage pools	77.10	2.48
Issuers of asset-backed securities less securitized Real Estate Investment Trusts (REITs)	616.50	19.80
Finance companies	58.10	1.87
Real Estate Investment Trusts (REITs)	34.80	1.12
Other	68.20	2.19
Total	$3,113.20	100.00%

Source: Board of Governors of the Federal Reserve, "Z. 1: Flow of Funds of the United States," press release, September 16, 2011, http://www.federalreserve.gov/releases/z1/Current/. Tables L. 219 and L. 220 and CRS calculations.

Note: Other includes households and nonprofit organizations, nonfarm nonfinancial, nonfarm noncorporate, property-casualty insurance companies, private pension funds, and state and local government retirement funds.

According to the National Council of Real Estate Investment Fiduciaries (NCREIF), investments in commercial real estate have had a positive rate of return between the first quarter of 2010 and the second quarter of 2011, following negative rates of return in the previous six quarters.[19]

Differences between Commercial and Residential Mortgages

The structure of commercial mortgages differs from that of residential mortgages (particularly for owner-occupied homes), reflecting different motivations for owning commercial and residential property. Commercial property is purchased as a business investment to earn a profit, whereas owner-occupied homes are purchased primarily for shelter.[20] If the rate of profit on a project is greater than the cost of borrowing, profitability can be increased—at the cost of increased risk— by increasing leverage, that is, by borrowing more of the money required to finance the project.

Although both commercial and residential mortgages facilitate the purchase of real estate, their terms differ from each other in a number of ways:

- First, commercial mortgages end with large balloon payments, whereas residential mortgages as a rule do not.[21]
- Second, commercial mortgages are typically for 7 to 10 years in contrast to 30 years for residential mortgages.
- Third, commercial mortgages usually prohibit or penalize prepayment, whereas most residential mortgages do not.
- Fourth, commercial mortgages are most frequently nonrecourse, which means that in the event of foreclosure, the borrower's liability is limited to the property; home mortgage recourse varies by state.[22]
- Fifth, commercial mortgages sometimes have reserve accounts to provide an additional buffer in the event of poor loan performance.

Commercial mortgages in the United States amount to $3.1 trillion compared with home mortgages of $10 trillion.[23]

One approach to financial analysis is to balance the risks and the profits of a potential investment. For example, a lender will seek a higher profit on riskier mortgages to compensate for the risk of a loss. When a specific potential borrower appears to present elevated risk levels, the lender will either quote a higher mortgage rate, add terms and conditions to reduce the risk, or in the extreme case, decline to make the loan.

The risk to a lender can be reduced by requiring the borrower to contribute more money to the purchase or by requiring some sort of credit enhancement, such as a third-party guarantee. In some situations, lending risk is reduced by making the loan for a shorter period of time.

Balloon payments in commercial mortgages occur because the borrower's payments do not fully amortize the loan. This allows the same amount of cash flow to support a larger mortgage and the real estate owner to purchase more property with the same assets. The balloon payments in commercial mortgages are sometimes called "soft bullets" and "hard bullets." A soft bullet allows the borrower to extend the life of the mortgage, perhaps at a higher interest rate, but a hard bullet does not allow extension. The interest rate on a mortgage with a soft bullet is typically higher than for an otherwise identical mortgage with a hard bullet. In the past, most soft bullets were paid on time. Lenders valued the higher interest rate they received on soft bullet mortgages, and borrowers valued the flexibility.

The shorter term for commercial mortgages coupled with prohibitions or penalties for prepayment provide both borrower and lender with greater cash flow certainty. Prepayments are a risk for lenders because borrowers tend to prepay when interest rates have declined, leaving the lender to replace the prepaid mortgage with a lower interest rate mortgage. In general, lenders prefer to make loans with contractual prohibitions on prepayments, expensive penalties for prepayments, or higher interest rates.

Residential borrowers usually can prepay without penalty, but commercial mortgages commonly require a borrower wishing to remove the lien on property (the equivalent of prepaying the mortgage) to give the lender U.S. Treasury bonds to match the cash flow of the mortgage.[24] (This is called defeasance.) This replaces the risky mortgage payments with riskless Treasury bonds paying the same interest rate; the borrower usually finds it more advantageous not to prepay.

In addition, the shorter mortgage life reduces the incentive for the borrower to prepay because there is less time to reap the benefits of the lower interest rate. The shorter mortgage life provides an opportunity for the property owner to increase leverage when refinancing.

The nonrecourse feature of most commercial mortgages shifts some of the costs of foreclosure from the borrower to the lender. In the event of foreclosure, if the property is sold for less than the amount owed, the lender has no further remedy. If a loan is made with recourse, the borrower (corporate or individual) is responsible for the balance owed.

Reserve accounts are often required for commercial mortgages and are an expansion of the escrow requirements that residential mortgages typically contain. In a similar manner, a homeowner makes monthly payments for property taxes and property insurance into an escrow account. A commercial reserve account may have these and payments for major items such as a new roof or heating, ventilation and air conditioning system. Sometimes these accounts are set based on the specific property, and sometimes a rule of thumb is employed using the property's rents or square footage.

Underwriting

Underwriting is the process of reviewing and analyzing the risks and potential profitability of a loan application. Basically, underwriting a loan application estimates the ability and willingness of the potential borrower to repay the loan on schedule, and the likely value of the collateral in the event that the borrower does not repay the loan.

The process of underwriting residential mortgages considers an applicant's income, history of paying previous loans, and the likely value of the home in the event of foreclosure. Commercial mortgage underwriting is similar, but differs with respect to the terms of the loan and the type of borrowers. Instead of considering the applicant's income, the income generated by the property is evaluated. The borrower's ability and willingness to repay the mortgage is considered. The likely value of the property in foreclosure is also considered. In addition, the terms of commercial mortgages are much less standardized so the risks that the borrower will not make all required mortgage payments are reviewed.

Both residential and commercial mortgages require professional appraisals. A residential appraisal usually is based on the sale of comparable homes in the area, but commercial property is frequently unique, necessitating a different approach. Typically, a commercial appraisal depends on an analysis of the market for similar property, the property's competitiveness within that market, and the property's ability to generate a cash flow to service the mortgage.

Two ratios are widely used in underwriting commercial mortgages: the debt service coverage ratio (DSCR) and the loan to value ratio (LTV). The DSCR is the annual net cash flow of the property divided by the annual principal and interest payments of the mortgage. For example, this cash flow might come from the rent paid by tenants. An application with a DSCR of more than 1.0 has more projected cash flow than required for paying the mortgage. In some cases such as acquisition, development and construction (ADC) loans, a lender will accept a DSCR below 1.0 if the borrower is willing to place additional funds in a reserve account. Most commercial mortgage underwriting considers mortgage terms, such as fixed or floating interest rates, when determining if a DSCR is adequate.

The DSCR is somewhat analogous to the front-end ratio or ratio of housing expenses to income for residential mortgages and measures the ability of a property to make its mortgage payments.

The LTV is a measure of how much collateral would be available in the event of a default. A lower LTV reflects a smaller loan on a more valuable property and a greater chance of recovery in the event of default. Both commercial and residential mortgages use the LTV. The maximum LTV on owner-occupied homes with mortgages insured by the Federal Housing

Administration (FHA) is 97%, and "conforming" residential mortgages with LTVs above 80% require credit enhancements such as borrower paid mortgage insurance. There are no comparable numbers for commercial mortgages, although a proposal to limit commercial mortgage LTVs to 75% was mentioned earlier.

In short, the DSCR is an indicator of the probability of default, and the LTV is a way to summarize the loss severity if a default occurs.

Since the peak of the housing boom, delinquency rates on tenant leases and tenant bankruptcies have increased. Because more tenants and renters are not paying their landlords, the property owners are unable to pay their mortgages. Echoing home prices, commercial property values have declined, and this has increased loss severity. **Figure 1** charts one measure of commercial prices from the fourth quarter of 2000 through the second quarter of 2011. It shows that commercial property prices were relatively constant in 2001, increased until the end of 2007, and declined sharply in 2008 and 2009. Apartments, retail, and industrial property prices doubled between the end of 2000 and 2007. Office property did not increase as much. Since the third quarter of 2009, commercial real estate prices changed little on average, but there has been large variation across the sectors. The overall commercial price pattern is similar to the changes in home prices.

COMMERCIAL MORTGAGE LENDING ISSUES

This section discusses the possible impact of commercial mortgage defaults on lenders.

Federally Insured Banks' Exposure to Commercial Mortgages

Table 2 shows that small FDIC-insured banks have, as a group, greater loan exposure in the areas of nonfarm nonresidential real estate (30% compared with 12% for large banks) and construction (7% compared with 3% for large banks). Construction loans frequently have severe losses if they default because there is a limited market for a partially developed real estate project.

If these loans become delinquent or go into foreclosure, these smaller banks would find their capital reduced. This, in turn, could lead the FDIC to seize the banks and dispose of their assets.

Fourth Quarter 2000 to Second Quarter 2011

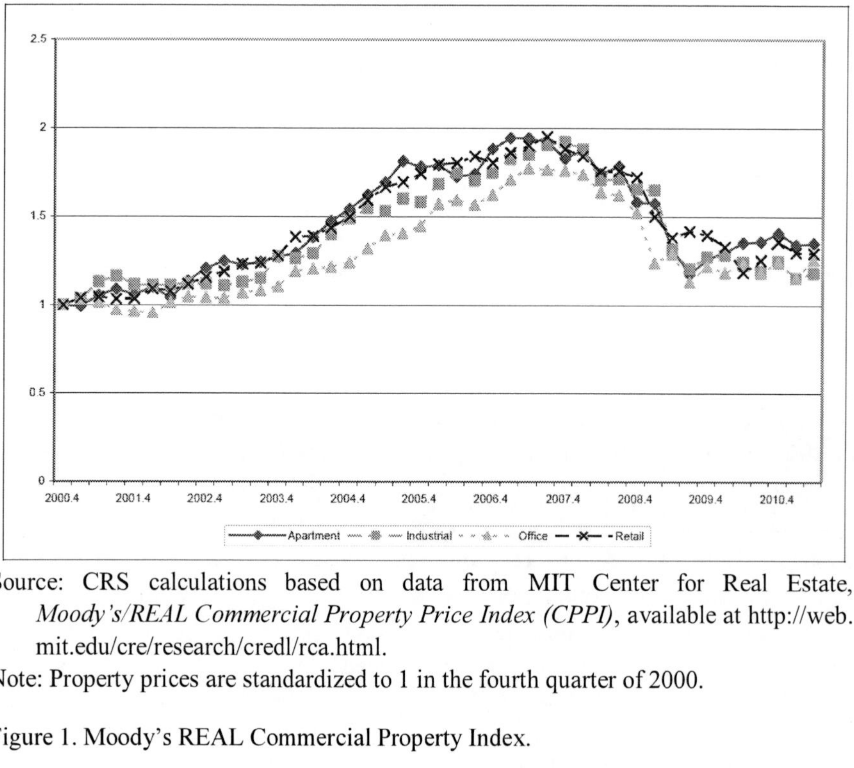

Source: CRS calculations based on data from MIT Center for Real Estate, *Moody's/REAL Commercial Property Price Index (CPPI)*, available at http://web.mit.edu/cre/research/credl/rca.html.

Note: Property prices are standardized to 1 in the fourth quarter of 2000.

Figure 1. Moody's REAL Commercial Property Index.

Table 2. Bank Portfolio Composition Second Quarter, 2011

Asset	Banks with Assets Less Than $1 Billion	Banks with Assets More Than $1 Billion	All Banks
Commercial and industrial loans	13%	18%	17%
Residential mortgages	27%	25%	25%
Nonfarm nonresidential real estate loans	30%	12%	14%
Credit cards	0%	10%	9%
Other consumer	4%	9%	8%
Agriculture	4%	0%	1%
Leases	0%	1%	4%
Construction	7%	3%	1%
All other loans	14%	21%	20%

Source: Federal Deposit Insurance Corporation, *FDIC Quarterly Banking Profile: All Institutions Graphs and Data Points*, Assets and Liabilities, June 30, 2011, available at http://www2.fdic.gov/qbp/index.asp.

The FDIC reported that at the end of the second quarter of 2011, 6.68% of real estate loans were noncurrent compared with 7.37% a year earlier.[25]

Commercial Mortgage-Backed Securities

Like residential mortgages, commercial mortgages are frequently pooled into MBS. MBS allow institutional lenders to supply mortgage money to borrowers throughout the nation, even if these lenders do not have the capability to issue the mortgage. In theory, this allows for specialization and economies of scale. Some businesses specialize in originating commercial mortgages, others in servicing the mortgages, and others, such as commercial banks, life insurance companies, savings institutions, CMBS issuers, and government-sponsored enterprises, in supplying the funds. Other businesses specialize in rating the CMBS.

CMBS, like residential mortgage-backed securities (RMBS), are typically created by sponsors that originate (or sometimes purchase) a mortgage and sell it to a trust that issues the CMBS. This creates a "bankruptcy remote" entity that should not be affected if the sponsor's financial condition includes bankruptcy.

CMBS, like RMBS, are typically divided into tranches or classes to better meet potential purchasers' risk, cash flow, diversification, and other preferences. One typical CMBS prospectus sought to raise $3.3 billion divided into 12 tranches ranging in size from $13 million to $1.2 billion.[26] The tranches had different expected lives, repayment of principal schedules, interest rates, and risk profiles.

In the above example, the CMBS was divided into three separate real estate mortgage investment conduits (REMICs), which are tax pass-throughs, meaning that the holders of the CMBS classes are taxed, but the REMIC is not taxed. Federal law and IRS regulations establish the rules that an MBS servicer must follow to be a REMIC. For example, to maintain their status as tax pass-throughs and to avoid being taxed, REMICs must be "passively" managed. Before the IRS issued Revenue Procedure 2009-45, an underlying mortgage could be modified only when "occasioned by default or a reasonably foreseeable default." IRS Revenue Procedure 2009-45 now allows servicers to modify mortgages before default if, "based on all the facts and circumstances, the holder or servicer reasonably believes that there is a significant risk of default of the pre-modification loan upon maturity of the loan or at an earlier date" without jeopardizing the REMIC's tax status.[27]

In addition, the contract between the MBS servicer and the investors (called the pooling and servicing agreement or PSA) could prevent modifications that the Revenue Procedures allow. A typical PSA prevents the servicers from modifying the underlying loans in ways that

- change the payment of principal or interest,
- impair the security of the loan, or
- reduce any credit enhancements.

Certain modifications are allowed if

- default is imminent,
- the modification could reduce losses on a mortgage, or
- the modification would not reduce credit enhancements.

CONCLUSION

Widespread evidence shows that commercial mortgage defaults and losses have been unusually high. More recently, it appears that there is some recovery, but this recovery varies across the nation and across various types of commercial mortgages. Some Members and others have expressed concerns that losses could increase, possibly weakening lenders, such as commercial banks and life insurance companies. These loan losses could result in contraction of credit to businesses and individuals and hinder the nation's economic recovery.

End Notes

[1] This report uses the term *commercial real estate* to mean all real estate except single-family homes and farms. Examples of commercial real estate are multifamily housing, shopping centers, medical buildings, and industrial property.

[2] Prabha Natarajan, "Delinquency Rate Rises for Mortgages—Commercial Borrowers Fall Behind," *Wall Street Journal*, January 8, 2009, p. C4 and Charles V. Bagli, "Huge N.Y. Housing Complex Is Returned to Creditors," *New York Times*, January 25, 2009, A12. The latter is available at http://www.nytimes.com/2010/01/25/nyregion/ 25stuy.html?hp.

[3] "Moody's: March CMBS Delinquencies Surge On Stuyvesant Town Loan," *Wall Street Journal,* http://online.wsj.com/article/SB10001424052748704723604575379543602271202.html?mod=dist_smartbrief.

[4] Fitch Ratings, "Ú.S. CMBS Market Trends," September 23, 2011, available at http://app.email.fitchratings.com/e/es.aspx?s=2404&e=5188&elq=418464a568664872bc2163fb0b76019e.

[5] Rebecca Christie and John McCormick, "Geithner Says Commercial Real Estate Woes Won't Spark Crisis," October 29, 2009, available at http://www.bloomberg.com/apps/news?pid=20601087&sid=aGGKUQhUZqaQ.

[6] U.S. Secretary of the Treasury, Timothy Geithner, *Written Testimony, Congressional Oversight Panel*, 111th Cong., 2nd sess., June 22, 2010, p. 2, available at http://www.treasury.gov/press-center/press-releases/Pages/tg754.aspx.

[7] Fitch Ratings, "U.S. CMBS Market Trends," September 23, 2011, available at http://app.email.fitchratings.com/e/es.aspx?s=2404&e=5188&elq=418464a568664872bc2163fb0b76019e.

[8] Mortgage Bankers' Association, *Mortgage Delinquency Rates for Major Investor Groups: Q1 2011*.

[9] U.S. Department of Treasury, Internal Revenue Service, "Modifications of Commercial Mortgage Loans Held by a Real Estate Mortgage Investment Conduit (REMIC)," *Internal Revenue Bulletin 2009-40*, October 5, 2009. See CRS Report R41226, *Loss Exposure and the Federal Deposit Insurance Corporation*, by Darryl E. Getter for information about the financial condition of the FDIC.

[10] Federal Deposit Insurance Corporation, "Assessments, Assessment Base and Rates," 75 *Federal Register* 72582-72609, November 24, 2010; Federal Deposit Insurance Corporation, "Proposed Assessment Rate Adjustment Guidelines for Large and Highly Complex Institutions," 76 *Federal Register* 21256-21265, April 15, 2011; and, Federal Deposit Insurance Corporation, "Assessments, Large Bank Pricing," 75 *Federal Register* 73983, November 30, 2010.

[11] Mortgage Bankers Association, *MBA Commercial Real Estate/Multifamily Finance Quarterly Databook: Q1 2011*, p. 69, http://www.mortgagebankers.org/files/Research/DataBooks/1Q11QuarterlyDatabook.pdf.

[12] Board of Governors of the Federal Reserve System, the Federal Deposit Insurance Corporation, the National Credit Union Administration, the Office of the Comptroller of the Currency, the Office of Thrift Supervision, and the Federal Financial Institutions Examination Council State Liaison Committee, *Policy Statement on Prudent Commercial Real Estate Loan Workouts*, October 30, 2009, available at http://www.fdic.gov/news/news/financial/2009/fil09061a1.pdf.

[13] Testimony of Kenneth T. Rosen, before the Financial Crisis Inquiry Commission, January 13, 2010, available at http://www.fcic.gov/hearings/pdfs/2010-0113-Rosen.pdf.

[14] CRS Report R40423, *Fair Value Accounting: Context and Current Concerns*, by Gary Shorter discusses mark-to-market issues in more detail.

[15] CRS Report R41427, *Troubled Asset Relief Program (TARP): Implementation and Status*, by Baird Webel.

[16] CRS Report RL34427, *Financial Turmoil: Federal Reserve Policy Responses*, by Marc Labonte

[17] Board of Governors of the Federal Reserve, "Federal Reserve System Monthly Report on Credit and Liquidity Programs and the Balance Sheet," September 2011, Table 9, p. 13, available at http://www.federalreserve.gov/monetarypolicy/files/monthlyclbsreport201109.pdf.

[18] Board of Governors of the Federal Reserve, "Z. 1: Flow of Funds of the United States," press release, September 16, 2011, p. 63, 97, available at http://www.federalreserve.gov/releases/z1/Current/.

[19] National Council of Real Estate Investment Fiduciaries, "NCREIF Property Index Returns," press release, Second Quarter 2011, http://www.ncreif.org/property-index-returns.aspx.

[20] Some home purchasers may have been motivated by the possibility of profits, but traditionally homes have been primarily for shelter and capital gains was an incidental motivation.

[21] Technically, commercial mortgages typically amortize over a period longer than the life of the mortgage leaving a balance to be paid at the end of the mortgage's term.

[22] For more details on residential mortgage recourse, see Andra C. Ghent and Marianna Kudlyak, *Recourse and Residential Mortgage Default: Theory and Evidence from U.S. States*, Federal

Reserve Bank of Richmond, No. 9'10, Richmond, VA, June 10, 2010, http://www.richmondfed.org/publications/research/working_papers/2009/pdf/wp09-10r.pdf.

[23] Board of Governors, Federal Reserve, "Z. 1 Flow of Funds," September 16, 2011, Tables L. 2117, available athttp://www.federalreserve.gov/releases/z1/Current/.

[24] Subprime mortgages usually prohibited prepayment.

[25] Federal Deposit Insurance Company, "FDIC Quarterly Banking Profile, Statistics at a Glance," press release, June 30, 2011, http://www.fdic.gov/bank/statistical/stats/2011jun/industry.html.

[26] Bear Stearns Commercial Mortgage, Inc., *Bear Stearns Commercial Mortgage Securities Trust 2004-TOP16*, June 11, 1004, available at http://edgar.sec.gov/Archives/edgar/data/908987/000095013604003372/file001.htm.

[27] Internal Revenue Service, "Revenue Procedure 2009-25," *Internal Revenue Bulletin: 2009-40*, October 5, 2009, available at http://www.irs.gov/irb/2009-40_IRB/ar01.html.

INDEX

D

E

F

G

H

I

J

L

M

N

O

P

Q

R

S

T

U

V

W

Y